QUICK BITES OF INSIGHT

MICRO-SIZED LEARNING ON WORK AND LEADERSHIP

RYAN MCCREA

Published by: Luci Leadership Consulting, LLC

Cover Design by: Susan McCrea

Illustrations by: Todd Bauman

ISBN Paperback: 979-8-9930711-0-7

ISBN eBook: 979-8-9930711-1-4

To every leader and team member I've had the privilege to learn from, thank you. Whether your guidance lit the way or pushed me to grow, you've each shaped my journey and helped me see things more clearly.

And to my loving wife, Susan: your steady support, patience, and belief in me have been the foundation of everything I've built. This book belongs to you as much as it does to me.

CONTENTS

PRAISE FOR QUICK BITES OF INSIGHT

"Ryan McCrea has whipped up the perfect snack for the soul of leadership - easy to digest, yet nourishing, rich and filling. Quick Bites of Insight™ proves that meaningful growth doesn't require hours of reading or grand gestures - just a few mindful minutes and the willingness to try something new."

-**Julie Winkle Giulioni**, Coauthor of Help Them Grow or Watch Them Go and Author of Promotions Are So Yesterday

"Quick Bites of Insight™ is a leadership playbook for today's world, delivering real talk, lively stories, and practical rituals that turn micro-moments into lasting growth; a refreshing, must-read toolbox for anyone ready to spark change in themselves and their teams, one powerful idea at a time."

-**Charles Good**, President, The Institute for Management Studies

"Quick Bites of Insight™ is an easy and engaging read, packed with practical wisdom that you can put into action right away. Ryan makes leadership development accessible by offering tangible and applicable steps that truly meet you where you are. This book is clear, actionable, and inspiring with tools you'll return to again and again. A genuine gift for anyone who wants to grow in life and leadership."

-**Justine Froelker, MEd, LPC**, Author, Speaker & Corporate Trainer

"I can only imagine the difference a leader would notice if they put just one of these quick bites into practice - let alone several of them. If you are a leader, or aspire to be one, I challenge you to 'take one bite' each week and try it out. That feels doable, and over time, I guarantee it will have a real impact on your life and the lives of your team."

-**Steph Auping,** Leadership Facilitator and Coach - Founder of Level Up Leadership

"Every leader should own and use this book! Each insight offers clear and actionable sparks of wisdom that are applicable at any stage of leadership. I found myself inspired, challenged, and reflective as I read through the book. I was reminded that small, intentional choices shape great leadership. This is a must-have resource for anyone looking to grow in their path as a leader with purpose and impact."

-**Diana Bentz, SPHR,** EVP, Chief Human Resources Officer, Bi-State Development

"Quick Bites of Insight is like a coach you can keep in your pocket, filled with actionable and relatable leadership stories. I love that the book is meant to be a real-time resource for leaders. Each quick bite is easy to read, digest, and sends you into action. I could see myself coming back to different insights to use as a quick way to get unstuck. Ryan beautifully weaves in his own experience as a leader with his stories as a coach and talent development professional."

-**Megan Galloway,** Founder, Everleader Consulting

"The world of work is evolving quickly. Quick Bites of Insight™ reminds us that leadership isn't about mastering change all at once, but it's about steady, small actions that build trust and clarity."

-**Al Dea**, Founder, The Edge of Work

"In Quick Bites of Insight™, Ryan does a great job giving high-impact, bite-sized pieces of leadership wisdom you can put to work every day."

-**Terence Bostic, Ph.D.**, Managing Partner at CMA Global

INTRODUCTION

I find people endlessly fascinating. Humans are complicated and inspiring in so many ways. My life's work has been about understanding people and helping to make the world a better place, and that has guided a fulfilling career in the people business.

My curiosity about the human experience showed up early. I asked a lot of questions and talked even more. I was absolutely that kid. I wanted to know what people were thinking and why they did what they did. I was a curious little booger, and I haven't changed much.

As I got older, I started really focusing on how people interacted, and I was especially intrigued with how certain people seemed to be natural leaders. I jumped into leadership roles, formal and informal, throughout my teen and high school years.

I hit my stride in college. I was a Resident Assistant on campus, President of Psi Chi, Program Director for our on-campus movie station, and a peer counselor. I took on various leadership roles and gathered experiences that informed me of who I would be and how I would impact the world.

College is also where I found a degree that matched what I cared about. Industrial Organizational Psychology. Don't worry, I yawned just writing it. What is it? Here is how I explain it. I am a business psychologist. I use what we know about human behavior and translate that into useful information to make people, teams, leaders and organizations better. I have been lucky to leverage my skillset with companies of all sizes, from non-profits all the way up to global Fortune 500 companies.

Helping people grow has always felt meaningful to me, whether it happens through a good conversation, a thoughtful question, or a new way of seeing something. Over the years, I've tried to share what I've learned by facilitating, coaching, mentoring, speaking on podcasts, writing articles, giving interviews, presenting at conferences, and every now and then posting on LinkedIn.

In 2025, I wanted to try something new. I wanted learning to feel easier and more manageable. Not everyone has time for a full book, but most people can spare a few minutes for something useful. That idea led to Quick Bites of Insight^{TM} .

Each week on LinkedIn, I shared short, action-focused reflections on leadership, learning, and the changing world of work. They were meant to be small, helpful moments people could grab in the middle of a busy life.

This book brings together a curated set of those insights. They've been expanded and organized to support you in the moments that matter. Whether you're leading others, growing in your career, or simply doing your best to navigate work life, I hope something here connects with you. Learning doesn't have to take a long time to make a difference.

MAKING MICROLEARNING WORK FOR YOU - BRINGING QUICK BITES OF INSIGHT TO LIFE

Growth doesn't require grand gestures. It happens through small, deliberate steps. Think of Quick Bites of Insight™ as a mirror and a compass. Let it help you see where you are and point to who you're becoming. Development isn't a destination. It's a daily practice.

Development doesn't just happen in a single workshop or by reading a book. It happens in the in-between moments in our real lives - the hallway conversations, the tricky email, the team meeting that went off the rails, or the unexpected feedback that you couldn't shake. Growth comes when we pause, reflect, and adapt, one day and one moment at a time.

That's where Quick Bites of Insight™ comes in. This collection isn't designed to be read from cover to cover or in one sitting. Think of it as a toolbox you can reach for when you need perspective, encouragement, or a bit of clarity. The stories are short on purpose, offering practical, actionable guidance in a few minutes. But, for these insights to move beyond good advice, and into lasting development, they need to become learned behaviors that are practiced and perfected. Like any other skill, these must be applied practically and utilized in a way that allows for personal growth to take place.

Here's how to make these quick bites part of your daily learning rhythm:

1. Don't Just Read - Reflect

Skimming an article and thinking "that's a good point" is a start but it's just the beginning. Real learning happens when you engage with an idea.

- After reading a bite, challenge yourself to reflect by asking:
    - *"Where does this show up in my day-to-day work?"*
    - *"How does this apply to me and my role?"*
    - *"What am I doing that's aligned or not aligned with this concept?"*
    - *"How might an outcome be different if I applied this idea?"*
    - *"What's one behavior I could shift based on the insight?"*

Reflection builds awareness, and awareness is the foundation of growth.

2. Practice How these Can Apply in the Flow of Work

The best learning is embedded in real life. Let each story act as a prompt for micro-experiments in your day. You don't need to overhaul your leadership style or work approach. You just need to try something small.

Examples:

- After reading an insight on listening, spend your next team meeting saying less and paraphrasing more.
- After reading an insight on managing up, take five minutes before your next manager touchpoint to clarify your key message.
- After reading about navigating conflict, choose one conversation this week to lean into instead of avoiding it.

Change doesn't need to be big to be meaningful. The goal is to experiment and do one thing differently and then reflect on how your micro-shifts in behavior are impacting the outcome.

3. Build a Ritual Around It

Learning sticks when it becomes a habit. Whether it's once a day, a week, or every Monday morning, build your own rhythm with this book.

You might:

- Keep the book on your desk and open it each morning.
- Use it as a weekly journaling prompt.
- Pair your reading with an established habit like a coffee break or end-of-day wrap-up.

Make it a small ritual, something you enjoy and look forward to, rather than just another task.

4. Make It Social

Leadership is not a solo sport. Learning in isolation limits growth, but learning with others magnifies and multiplies it. Use these insights to start conversations with your team, your peers, or your mentor.

Ways to do that:

- Share a favorite story at your next team meeting and ask, "What would this look like for us?"
- Send a relevant article to a colleague and say, "This reminded me of our recent challenge. What do you think?"
- Use a chapter as a warm-up question in your next leadership huddle or one-on-one.

When we learn out loud, we grow faster and bring others along with us on the journey of growth.

5. Track What Matters

One of the best ways to turn learning into behavior is to track it - not for perfection, but for progress. Keep a simple learning journal or digital note where you capture:

- Key takeaways from what you read
- Small actions you tried
- Wins, misses, and lessons learned

Revisiting your own reflections over time can reveal patterns, spark new ideas, and build your personal leadership roadmap.

6. Revisit and Reframe Often

This book is *not* meant to be read once and shelved. It's meant to be revisited. As your context shifts around new projects, new roles, and new challenges, your interpretation of each insight will also shift.

That story on delegation? It'll land differently when you're managing a larger team. The discussion about resilience? It might hit harder after a tough quarter.

Come back to these pages often. Mark the ones that stand out to you. Reread them with a new perspective. Growth comes in cycles and what didn't seem relevant before might be just what you need now.

7. Coach Yourself Through the Insights

Each story can serve as a mini coaching session. Read with a coach's mindset by asking:

- *What's the challenge or opportunity here?*
- *What do I notice about myself as I read this?*
- *What's one courageous step I could take next?*

You don't need to wait for formal coaching to start developing yourself. With curiosity and intention, every insight becomes a tool for self-guided growth.

Final Word: You Don't Need to Be Perfect - Just Present

Leadership is something you practice, not just perform. The goal isn't to master every idea in this book. It's to become more aware, try new things, and grow a bit each day.

Quick Bites of Insight™ was designed to meet you where

you are, whether you're just getting started in your leadership journey or you've been at it for decades. It's here to remind you that small shifts can lead to lasting transformation.

Take a breath. Read one story. Try one thing. Reflect one time. Growth lives in ordinary moments, made extraordinary by your intention.

Let's keep growing. One bite at a time.

COLLABORATION AND COMMUNICATION

Great teams don't just happen; they're built through intentional habits, clear communication, and trust. This collection focuses on the everyday skills that help people work better together.

INSIGHT #1 – SAYING NO WITHOUT BURNING BRIDGES

Let me tell you something that took me way too long to learn early on in my career:

- *You can say "no" without being a jerk.*
- *You can set a boundary and still be kind.*
- *You can protect your time without damaging your relationships.*

For years, I said yes to almost everything. Extra projects, late meetings, last minute favors. Even when I knew I didn't have the time. I wanted to be helpful, to be seen as a team player, and to avoid disappointing anyone.

But here's what I finally learned. Saying no respectfully, at the right time, is a sign of leadership. Not selfishness.

Here are five practical ways to say "no" without burning bridges:

Lead with Gratitude – Start by acknowledging the opportunity or the person's trust in you. "Thanks for thinking of me for this, I really appreciate it."

Be Clear and Kind – No one benefits from a vague maybe. It's okay to say no. Just be direct and thoughtful. "This isn't something I can take on right now without compromising other priorities."

Explain Briefly (But Don't Over-Apologize) – You don't owe a long backstory. A short explanation helps them understand your decision. "I'm currently focused on X, and I want to give it my full attention."

4 **Offer an Alternative if You Can** - Can you suggest another person, resource, or later time? "I can't join this round, but I'd be happy to review the plan before launch."

5 **Stay future-focused -** Make it clear that your "no" is situational, not personal. "Please keep me in mind for future opportunities. I'd love to support when I can."

You can say no and still be seen as collaborative, professional, and kind. You're not rejecting people. You're just protecting your capacity. And that's not only okay, but it's also smart.

INSIGHT #2 - CREATING CONDITIONS FOR COLLABORATION THAT STICK

On paper, collaboration seems simple. If I had a dollar for every time I was called in to try to help teams collaborate better together, I would be rich! The reality is that collaboration doesn't just happen, it's built. It's built by leaders who choose to create the conditions for it.

If you're looking to drive more collaboration across your organization, here are 5 practical shifts you can make right now:

- **Create "Collision Points"** – Look for ways to create intentional moments where teams cross paths. Monthly cross-functional standups, project showcases, or lunch and learns can spark ideas and build relationships. These moments become even more powerful when you connect them to shared goals.
- **Clarify the Why Behind the Work** – People collaborate more when they understand how their work connects to something bigger. Start meetings by grounding the team in the purpose of the work and the impact you are trying to make. Share the endgame, not just the task list.
- **Reward the Team, not Just the Hero** – When recognition only goes to the person who crosses the finish line, collaboration dries up. Make it a point to celebrate the partnerships that made the outcome possible. Shine a light on the co-creators.

- **Bust the Silos. Don't Simply Manage Around Them** – Encourage job shadowing, rotate people into new spaces, and normalize asking for input outside your lane or department. Silos shrink when people know each other and curiosity becomes part of the culture.
- **Model it. Obsessively** – Leaders who seek input, celebrate others, and co-create solutions don't just talk collaboration, they live it. Your example is your loudest message.

If you want more collaboration, build more connection. Stop waiting for alignment to magically appear. Create it, moment by moment.

INSIGHT #3 – WANT BETTER FEEDBACK? ASK BETTER QUESTIONS

One of the most powerful ways to grow in your career isn't waiting for your annual review. It's learning how to ask for feedback in a way that invites honesty and helps you actually get better.

Most people want to give helpful feedback. They just don't always know how, especially if your ask is too broad or vague. Instead of "Do you have any feedback for me?" (cue awkward silence), try:

- "What's one thing I could do differently next time to be more effective?"

- "Where do you think I missed the mark on that project?"
- "What's something I'm doing well that I should keep doing?"

These questions make it easier for others to be honest, specific, and constructive. And they show that you're not just open to feedback, but you invite it.

But asking is only half the work. The other half is how you respond. When someone shares feedback, especially the kind that stings a bit, resist the urge to explain, defend, or minimize. Pause. Listen. Say thank you. Even tough feedback usually points to something useful.

Responding with openness shows emotional maturity and a real commitment to growth. It also encourages people to keep giving you the kind of insight that helps you improve.

When you consistently ask for feedback and receive it with curiosity instead of defensiveness, you don't just improve your performance. You build trust. You model growth. You become the kind of teammate people want to work with.

Feedback isn't a threat. It is a gift. And sometimes the strongest move you can make is to ask for it and accept it with courage and humility.

INSIGHT #4 – TEAM NORMS THAT SURVIVE MONDAY MORNING

There's something incredibly powerful about a team that just clicks. When expectations are clear, accountability feels natural and everyone shows up not just for the work, but for each other.

That magic doesn't happen by accident.

- It's built.
- It's practiced.
- And it starts with team norms.

Team norms are the shared agreements about how we work together. They are more than meeting cadence or email etiquette. They get into the heart of team dynamics. How we give feedback, how we make decisions, how we communicate when things get tense, and how we celebrate the wins that matter.

Most team norms fall flat. They are created in a one-off meeting, documented in a Google Doc… and never mentioned again.

How do you build team norms that stick? Explore these strategies that can make all the difference:

Co-create, Do Not Dictate – Invite your team to reflect on what great teamwork looks like for them. One of the most powerful ways to do this is by co-creating a team charter: a shared agreement or "team contract" that outlines how you'll work together, communicate, and support one another. Use a team meeting to explore what helps each person feel safe, respected, and energized. This isn't just a checklist, it's a chance to shape your team's culture together.

- **Make them Visible –** Norms should live in the work, not in a forgotten folder. Revisit them at the start of meetings. Bring them into retros. Put them somewhere visible, even if your team is fully remote.
- **Normalize Revisiting and Refining –** Team dynamics shift. People come and go. What worked last quarter might not serve you today. Set a cadence to reflect, assess, and evolve your norms as a team.
- **Model and Reinforce Consistently –** How you show up matters. Call out moments where someone lives the norm. Gently address it when something feels off. Culture is created by what we tolerate and what we celebrate.
- **Use Real-Life Scenarios –** Skip the vague statements. Bring your norms to life. Instead of saying "assume good intent," try something more practical, like "When someone shows up late, check in before making assumptions." Define your values and give examples of what good and not-so-good look like in action.

Why does this matter so much to me? Early in my career, I was part of a team that struggled. Miscommunication, missed expectations, and a general sense of "what are we even doing?" It wasn't a talent issue. It was an alignment issue.

I remember thinking, we spend most of our waking hours together. Why wouldn't we be intentional about how we work?

That experience lit a fire in me to understand what makes teams thrive. Helping teams build strong, healthy, human-centered ways of working is not just work for me. It is personal.

Because when a team thrives, people thrive. And that is the kind of ripple effect I want to be part of every day.

INSIGHT #5 – IS YOUR FEEDBACK FUELING GROWTH OR CRUSHING POTENTIAL?

Leaders, feedback isn't just an item on your to-do list. It's one of the most powerful tools in your leadership arsenal. When done right, it inspires growth, strengthens trust, and drives performance. When done poorly, it creates confusion, frustration, and stagnation.

The question is: How effective is *your* feedback?

Too often, feedback is vague, overly critical, or delayed to the point of irrelevance. That's not feedback, it's noise.

Here's the challenge: Stop being "nice." Start being clear, because clear is kind. Great leaders don't sugarcoat, avoid, or soften the message to keep things comfortable. They care enough to be direct but thoughtful. They provide feedback that's:

- **Specific** - What exactly worked or did not work? Give specific examples.
- **Actionable** – What's the next step? What needs to change, how and when?
- **Timely** – Don't wait for the next performance review to address an issue or celebrate a win. If it is important, it shouldn't wait.
- **Balanced** – Celebrate the strengths while addressing the opportunities. Positive feedback can have an outsized impact on performance. Catch people doing something right and they are likely to repeat it.

Feedback is not just about delivering a message. It is a

conversation. It is a chance to create an environment where your team feels safe to ask questions, clarify expectations, and own their development.

The best leaders don't just give feedback. They teach through feedback. They make it a tool for growth, not a weapon for critique.

I'll leave you with this:

- *When was the last time you gave feedback that truly moved the needle for someone?*
- *Are you delivering feedback that's clear, productive, and empowering?*
- *How would your team describe your feedback style?*
- *How can you elevate your feedback game this year?*

Your team is waiting for clarity, insight, and growth. The question is, will you give it to them?

INSIGHT #6 – PSYCHOLOGICAL SAFETY: WHAT IT LOOKS LIKE IN ACTION

We talk about psychological safety a lot in leadership and team development but what does it look like in action?

At its core, psychological safety means people feel safe to speak up, take risks, admit mistakes, and be themselves, without fear of embarrassment, rejection, or punishment. It's not about avoiding conflict or being "nice" all the time. It's about creating an environment where people feel respected and safe to be real. Simply stated, it's trust at scale.

When psychological safety is present, teams thrive. When it is missing, innovation and engagement drop fast.

Here are a few ways to build psychological safety in practical, everyday moments:

- **Normalize Asking for Help** - Say things like "I don't know - what do you think?" or "I'd love a second set of eyes on this." This signals that vulnerability is not a weakness, it's collaboration.
- **Respond, Don't React** – When someone brings forward a concern, your first response matters. Pause, thank them, and get curious. "Thanks for bringing that up. Can you tell me more?" goes a long way.
- **Interrupt Interruptions** – If someone gets talked over in a meeting, step in gently: "I want to hear what Taylor was saying before we move on." It shows everyone that all voices matter.
- **Celebrate Smart Risks, Even When They Don't Pan Out** – When someone tries something new and it does not pan out, recognize the effort. "I appreciate you trying something different. That is the kind of thinking we need." You teach the team that creativity beats perfection.
- **Model Learning Out Loud** – Share what you've learned from a failure or misstep. It helps others feel less pressure to be perfect.

People will do amazing things when they feel safe, seen, and supported.

If you're a leader (formal or informal), ask yourself:

- *Am I creating a space where people feel safe to speak up?*
- *Do I model the behavior I hope to see?*
- *When people take risks, do I reward it or retreat?*

Psychological safety isn't a one-time initiative. It's a daily commitment to leading with empathy, curiosity, and courage.

Let's keep building workplaces where people can bring their full selves to the table. That's where people and teams truly thrive.

13

INSIGHT #7 – ASKING BETTER QUESTIONS IN MEETINGS: SIX TIPS TO CONTRIBUTE WITHOUT DERAILING THE FLOW

We've all been in *that* meeting. The one where someone asks a question so off-track, so oddly timed, or so long-winded that you can feel the oxygen leave the room.

But questions matter. The right question, asked at the right moment, can create clarity, build trust, and keep a meeting moving in the direction it's supposed to go.

Here are six practical ways to ask better questions in meetings. Ones that add value, not derail momentum:

1. **Anchor Your Question in the Goal of the Meeting -** Before speaking up, ask yourself: "How does this question help move us closer to the purpose of this meeting?" If it doesn't connect, consider parking it for later.

2. **Lead with Curiosity, not Critique** – Instead of "Why didn't we do it this way?" try "What was the thinking behind the current approach?" Tone and intention matter. People respond better when they don't feel on the defense.

3. **Time it Right** – Every meeting has a rhythm. Jumping in with questions mid-sentence or during a momentum surge can sidetrack the flow. Jot it down and wait for a natural pause or designated discussion time.

4. **Be Brief and Clear** – Make your question easy to answer. Rambling loses people. Clarity shows respect for everyone's time.

5. **Consider your Audience** – Ask questions that elevate shared understanding, not ones that spotlight what you already know. Meetings aren't a stage, they're for a collaboration.

6. **Follow-up Outside the Meeting When Needed.** Not every question needs to be answered right now. If it's specific, complex, or off topic, follow up one-on-one afterward. That shows respect and initiative.

The best contributors in meetings don't always say the most, they ask the right questions at the right time. Let's be those people.

INSIGHT #8 - MICRO INCLUSIONS: SMALL ACTS THAT BUILD BELONGING

Ever been the odd person out on a team?

I have. Early in my career, I joined a group where everyone already knew the inside jokes, the unspoken rules, even the "usual seats" in the meeting room. No one was unkind, but no one noticed that I wasn't part of the flow yet. It felt a little like walking into a party where everyone is settled in and there's no space on the couch.

That experience stuck with me, and it reminds me just how important inclusion is.

Inclusion isn't about big speeches or company-wide celebrations. It's built in the small, consistent moments that say, "You matter here." I call these micro inclusions. Simple, intentional actions that help people feel seen, heard, and part of the team.

And they make a real difference. When people feel included, trust grows, collaboration gets easier, and results get better. When they don't have to wonder if they belong, they can focus on doing their best work.

Want to build inclusion into your team culture? Start small. Try this:

✓ **Rotate Meeting Leadership** – Don't let the same person own the room every time.

✓ **Use Names** – "Great idea, Jasmine" is ten times more powerful than "Yeah, that's good."

✓ **Invite Quieter Voices** – "Alex, we haven't heard from you yet, any thoughts?"

✓ **Recognize Effort, Not Just Outcomes** – Especially when someone takes a risk or steps outside their comfort zone.

✓ **Watch Side Conversations** – If it's not for everyone, it might make someone feel left out. These micro inclusions don't take much time but over time, they build psychological safety, trust, and the kind of culture where people thrive.

✓ **Be Curious About Differences** – When someone offers a different perspective, respond with "Tell me more" instead of defaulting to debate.

✓ **Avoid Assumptions About Availability** – Don't guess who can stay late, travel, or attend after-hours events. Ask.

✓ **Invite Feedback on Team Norms** – Ask, "What's one thing we could do to make this team feel more inclusive?" Act on what you hear.

Because belonging is not built in big, rare moments. It's built in small ones. Over and over again.

INSIGHT #9 – LISTENING TO UNDERSTAND

I'll be honest, I still struggle with listening to understand.

Sometimes, when I'm listening to someone in a meeting or one-on-one, I catch myself already drafting my response in my head instead of truly hearing what they're saying. It's not because I don't care. It's because I care too quickly.

But listening to understand (not just respond) is one of the most underrated leadership skills we can build. When we slow down and really tune in, we catch what isn't being said, we ask better questions, and we make people feel seen and heard.

Here are a few ways I'm working on this:

- **Pause Before Replying** – Give it a second after they finish speaking. It shows you are thinking, not just reacting.
- **Don't Finish Their Sentence (Even in Your Head)** – Stay curious instead of trying to predict where they're going. You might be surprised where they go.
- **Ask Follow-Up Questions** – Try "Can you tell me more about that?" or "What do you need most right now?" instead of jumping to solve or shift the topic.
- **Listen with Your Body** – Nod. Uncross your arms. Lean in slightly. Give your full attention. These physical cues help you stay present and show the speaker you're engaged.
- **Drop the Mental Mic** – Even if you've got the

"perfect" response ready, let it go for a second. Focus on them, not how insightful you're about to be.

- **Reflect Back What You Heard** – A quick, "So what I'm hearing is…" can work wonders. It gives them a chance to clarify and shows you're actively tracking.
- **Remind Yourself: It's Not a Debate** – Most conversations aren't about winning, they're about connecting. That shift in mindset can change everything.

Real listening builds trust. Trust strengthens teams, relationships, and the decisions we make together.

Let's keep getting a little better at this, one conversation at a time.

INSIGHT #10 – RAISE YOUR HAND, THEN RAISE THE BAR

This one is tough, and maybe even a little uncomfortable. We need to normalize asking for help at work.

It sounds simple. But in reality? It's hard. Even I find it hard. I have the scars to show from not asking for help through the years.

Asking for help can make even the most confident person

feel exposed. It can feel like admitting we are not capable or not enough. Protecting our ego is baked deep into how we operate as humans. We all want to be seen as competent. So, we stay quiet. We tell ourselves we should already know this. We try to figure it out alone.

But asking for help is not weakness. It is strength. It is humility. It is what a growth mindset looks like in real life.

When we create cultures where people feel safe to raise their hand and say "I don't know," or ask for clarity, everybody wins. Collaboration improves. Learning accelerates. Trust deepens.

How do we build that kind of culture?

- **Leaders Go First** – If you're in a position of influence, model it. Say "I need your help," or "I'm not sure, what do you think?" Showing vulnerability gives others permission to do the same.
- **Respond with Appreciation, Not Judgment** – When someone asks for help, thank them for trusting you. Make it a moment of connection, not judgement or correction.
- **Build Psychological Safety Intentionally.** – Set the tone in meetings by reminding people that no one is expected to know everything. Questions are welcome. Curiosity is welcome.
- **Celebrate it Publicly** – If someone spoke up and asked for help that led to a breakthrough or better outcome, highlight it! Normalize the behavior by reinforcing it.
- **Rethink Onboarding** – Make it clear from day one that asking for help is expected and respected, not a last resort.

Let's redefine competence. It's not about having all the answers. It's about being confident enough to ask the right questions.

INSIGHT #11 - MASTERING THE ART OF MANAGING UP: A SKILL EVERYONE NEEDS

One of the most underrated leadership skills is not about leading teams or delivering projects. It is about how you lead and influence the people who lead you. It takes time to build this skill, and it often requires a shift in how we think about our work. I will admit, I did not fully understand it until the second half of my career.

And let me say this clearly. Managing up is not sucking up. It is not flattery and it is not manipulation. It is about building strong, healthy, and productive relationships with your leaders so you can create impact, accelerate your growth, and help your team thrive.

So, how do you do it? Here are three essential skills every professional, at any level, should master to effectively manage up:

Anticipate Needs Before They Arise – Great leaders value team members who are proactive. Pay attention to your leader's priorities, communication and work style, and stress points. Anticipate what they need before they ask, and you'll instantly position yourself as a trusted partner.

Communicate with Clarity and Confidence – Leaders don't have time to decode vague messages. Be clear, concise, and solutions focused. Instead of saying, "I ran into a problem," try, "I ran into a challenge, and here are two possible solutions. What do you think?"

Align with Their Goals and Make Them Look Good – Your leader's success is your success. Understand their objectives, align your work to their vision, and find ways to make their job easier. The more you help them succeed, the more opportunities will come your way.

23

Managing up is a skill that separates good employees from indispensable ones. It builds trust, strengthens influence, and opens doors to new opportunities.

CAREER DEVELOPMENT AND GROWTH

Career growth isn't a ladder. It's a series of choices, pivots, and learning moments. These ideas are meant to help people take ownership of their path and move forward with purpose.

INSIGHT #12 – THE 70% ZONE: WHERE DEVELOPMENT LIVES

Leaders, if you want to develop your team, the best classroom isn't a conference room. It's the work they do every day.

The 70/20/10 model is a simple guide for professional growth. Seventy percent comes from hands-on experience, twenty percent from relationships and feedback, and ten percent from formal learning. It is a reminder that real development happens in the flow of work and not only in a classroom.

Growth does not happen by accident. It happens when leaders create opportunities for their people to stretch, experiment, and take on challenges that push them beyond what feels easy. I have always tried to be intentional about finding those experiences. I once had someone on my team who wanted to sharpen her strategic skills. We found an opportunity for her to build the strategy for a newer piece of software, and it changed the way she saw her own potential.

Here's how you can harness the power of the 70% to develop your team:

Delegate with Development in Mind – Instead of keeping high-visibility or complex projects for yourself, pass them to your team members. Let them do the work while you provide guidance and support. Don't just hand over anything. Make sure it will give them the challenge they need. Be thoughtful and targeted.

Encourage Strategic Risk-Taking – Growth happens in the stretch zone, not the comfort zone. Give employees the freedom to test ideas, experiment, solve problems, and even make mistakes (because that's where real learning happens).

Rotate Responsibilities – Expose your team to different aspects of the business by cross-training, job shadowing, or project-based assignments. The more they experience, the more adaptable and capable they become.

Turn Challenges into Coaching Moments – When employees struggle with a task, don't jump in to fix it. Help them think through solutions. Ask, "What's another way to approach this?" or "What did you learn that you'll apply next time?" Learning is accelerated when reflection is part of the process.

Make Feedback a Habit – Regular, in-the-moment

feedback helps employees connect their actions to outcomes. Whether it's a quick debrief after a meeting or a shoutout for a job well done, real-time feedback fuels growth.

Most people do not need another training session. They need experiences that stretch them, challenges that grow them, and leaders who trust them enough to let them learn through real work.

INSIGHT #13 – CAREER CLARITY THROUGH CONVERSATION

Earlier in my career, people often came to me feeling stuck. They weren't lacking talent or drive. They were lacking direction. Many didn't even know what they truly wanted, yet they were looking at me for answers. That pushed me to think more deeply about how I could guide them, and it led me to the power of a thoughtful career conversation.

One of the most effective tools I've used for years is a curated set of reflection questions. These aren't just prompts. They're catalysts. They help people uncover what matters most, what energizes them, and where they want to grow next.

Here are some of the questions I've found most powerful in helping both leaders and team members gain direction:

- **What principles guide how you make decisions at work?** – This helps align choices with what feels authentic and fulfilling.
- **What kind of work makes you feel most alive?** – Whether it's solving problems, building relationships, or creating something new, this question helps pinpoint your energy sources.
- **What types of challenges do you enjoy tackling?** – Not all problems are created equal. Knowing which ones excite you can shape your future roles.
- **What work do you naturally gravitate toward and which do you avoid?** – This insight helps you design a

role that plays to your strengths and minimizes energy drains.

- **Where do you feel most confident and where do you feel stretched?** – Self-awareness is key to growth. This question helps you identify areas for development and celebration.
- **Are there strengths you rely on so heavily they sometimes get in your way?** – Even our best traits can become blind spots. This question invites balance.
- **What new capabilities are you eager to build?** – Growth is ongoing. This question keeps your development focused and intentional.
- **What kind of impact do you want to have in your work?** – Whether it's mentoring others, driving innovation, or improving systems, this question helps clarify your purpose.
- **How do you define career fulfillment?** – Success looks different for everyone. This question helps you articulate what it means for you.
- **Do you feel stretched and supported in your current role?** – Growth happens at the edge of comfort, but support makes it sustainable.
- **What kind of legacy do you want to leave behind?** – This long-view question helps connect your day-to-day work to a broader sense of meaning.
- **Who inspires you professionally and why?** – This question can reveal aspirations, values, and hidden goals.

These questions aren't magic. The conversation is. When we create space for honest reflection, we unlock potential. If you're a leader, a mentor, or just someone who wants to grow, start here. Ask one of these questions today. You might be surprised where it leads.

INSIGHT #14 – SHARE YOUR WINS WITHOUT FEELING WEIRD ABOUT IT

I can't count how many incredibly talented people I coach who tell me the same thing: "I'm just not comfortable talking about my own accomplishments."

They downplay their wins. They hesitate to share what's going well. And they almost always follow it up with, "I don't want to come off as too self-promoting."

Not sharing your impact doesn't make you humble. It often makes you invisible. And that invisibility? It can quietly derail your career trajectory.

I get it. It can feel awkward to spotlight your success, especially when you're wired to be collaborative, not competitive. But you can make your work visible without crossing into ego or self-promotion. It's not about bragging. It's about clarity, credibility, and connection.

Here are a few ways to do it more comfortably and effectively:

Share the "We" Before the "Me" – Give credit for the team effort, but don't leave your role out. "Our team just wrapped up a major customer experience initiative. I led the strategy and rollout, and I'm so proud of how we elevated our service ratings by 20%."

Focus on Outcomes, not Adjectives – Instead of saying you're "great at project management," say "Delivered a cross-functional initiative two weeks early and $40K under budget." Let the results speak for themselves. When possible, use numbers to stay objective while communicating concrete results.

Use Story, Not Spotlight – People connect through stories. Instead of dropping bullet-point achievements, share a quick behind-the-scenes look: "Six months ago, this project felt impossible. But we stuck with it, navigated a few surprises, and launched ahead of schedule."

Offer Value, Not Just Victory - Frame your share around what others might learn or take away. "Here's what worked for us and what I'd do differently next time." That's leadership, not ego.

Ask for feedback, not just attention – Try, "We just completed our project roadmap for the year. Would love to hear what's working for others in this space." You're sharing, but inviting others in.

The bottom line is simple. You can be one of your best advocates. Not by shouting, but by sharing with clarity, generosity, and intention.

INSIGHT #15 – MENTORSHIP AND SPONSORSHIP: KNOW THE DIFFERENCE, BUILD THE BRIDGE

I've had incredible mentors throughout my career. People who offered their time, their wisdom, and their honest feedback when I needed it most.

But I've also had sponsors, those rare individuals who not only coached me but spoke my name in rooms I wasn't in.

Here's the key difference:

Mentorship is about Development – A mentor helps you sharpen your skills, navigate challenges, and grow with confidence. It's guidance, encouragement, and insight.

Sponsorship is about Opportunity – A sponsor actively advocates for you, recommends you for stretch roles, and puts their reputation on the line to help accelerate your path.

Here's the truth we don't talk about enough: Sponsorship often starts with mentorship, but it doesn't start as sponsorship.

Why? Because sponsorship requires deep trust. Before someone will stake their name on your potential, they need to know your work, your values, and how you show up consistently.

They need to know you will do the work and own your part.

- If you're a mentor, ask yourself: Have I seen enough of this person in action to open a door for them?
- If you're being mentored, remember: The goal isn't to "get" a sponsor. It's to build real relationships where sponsorship can naturally grow.

Let's stop treating sponsorship like a transactional ask. Let's treat it like the outcome of trust, credibility, and shared belief in someone's future. Where mentorship is given, sponsorship is earned.

When that kind of trust is earned and given, careers can change in an instant.

INSIGHT #16 – CULTIVATING YOUR DEVELOPMENT GARDEN

During my time in learning and development, I've talked with thousands of people about their careers. One metaphor I always come back to is the garden. It's simple, but it sticks, because personal and professional growth works a lot like tending to a garden. Nothing flourishes overnight. It takes intention, care, and the right conditions to grow something meaningful.

It works because growth isn't instant. It's not linear. And it rarely happens the way we expect. Development looks less like a straight ladder and more like seasons, soil, storms, sunlight, pruning, and patience.

To cultivate your potential, you need four essential elements:

The Desire to Grow – Seeds don't sprout unless they're planted with purpose. Growth is intentional, sometimes slow, and often uncomfortable. But if you keep showing up, watering your goals with effort and patience, you'll see progress. *Ask yourself: What am I planting on purpose right now?*

The Nutrients – Soil alone won't grow a garden. You need to enrich it. That means building new capabilities, whether it's leading, influencing, communicating, or coaching. Your skills are the nutrients that fuel your development. *Ask yourself: What skill am I actively enriching right now? And what am I neglecting?*

The Right Conditions – Plants need sunlight, water, and space. You need feedback, coaching, stretch assignments, and learning experiences that challenge and support you. These are the conditions that help you thrive. *Ask yourself: What conditions help me thrive? And which ones do I need to adjust?*

The Community Around You – No garden grows in isolation. Surround yourself with mentors, peers, and leaders who encourage your growth, offer guidance, and help you navigate when things get tangled or unclear. *Ask yourself: Who is helping me tend my garden? And who do I need to invite in?*

Whether you're just planting seeds or tending a garden in full bloom, take a moment to reflect:

- *Am I still committed to growing?*
- *What skill do I need to cultivate next?*
- *What resources are helping me thrive?*
- *Who's helping me tend this garden?*

Your growth is already underway. With care, it will flourish in ways you may not even see coming.

INSIGHT #17 – THE POWER OF SMALL WINS: FUELING MOTIVATION AND MOMENTUM

Ever felt stuck at the start of a big project or goal? You're not alone. We've all stared at a blank page wondering what to do next.

The truth is that progress creates motivation. Not the other way around. People talk about writing blocks all the time. The best way to move past one is to keep writing. The same idea applies to almost anything we want to achieve.

This is where small wins come in. They are the quiet fuel behind performance, confidence, and momentum.

When we break a big goal into smaller, doable steps and celebrate those steps, we build a steady rhythm of progress. That rhythm builds motivation. That motivation becomes momentum. And momentum can move mountains.

Here are a few practical ways to harness the power of small wins, for yourself, your team, or your organization:

Shrink the Starting Line - Instead of launching into a massive project, identify the first micro-action. One email. One brainstorm. One slide. Progress starts with movement, not perfection.

Stack Visible Progress - Use checklists, kanban boards, or visual trackers to see your momentum build. Seeing progress is energizing.

Celebrate (Even Tiny) Victories - Don't wait until the finish line to cheer. Recognize and name small wins along the way. Do it during meetings, team updates, or even a quick Slack message. Recognition builds resilience.

✅ **Gamify the Grind** - Turn repetition into motivation. Score streaks, hit milestones, or unlock mini-rewards. It's not just fun, it's scientifically proven to be motivating.

✅ **Reflect Weekly** – Start your week with a quick reflection: What progress did I make last week? You'll often realize you're moving forward, even when you feel stuck.

Small wins may not be flashy, but they are foundational. They keep teams energized, leaders focused, and goals within reach.

INSIGHT #18 – INTENTIONAL FLEXIBILITY IN DEVELOPMENT

One of the most powerful ways to own your career is by being intentionally flexible.

So what does that actually mean?

When it comes to our development, we have to own our path. Doing great work matters, but it isn't always enough if we want to grow, move forward, or take on something new. And honestly, waiting for someone to tap you on the shoulder and say "you're ready" might never happen.

Being intentional means knowing what you want and actively seeking the skills and experiences that support that direction. It means being clear about where you want to go.

This is where flexibility comes in.

On any career journey, you will run into roadblocks. You will also get opportunities you never saw coming. You may be asked to take on something that feels uncomfortable or completely outside your plan. That isn't a sign to back away. It's usually the signal that it's time to stretch, because real growth rarely shows up in the comfort zone.

Many of the leaders I've met who truly thrive did not follow a neat, predictable path. A mentor encouraged them to try something new. A peer challenged their thinking. A leader saw potential they hadn't recognized. They stayed open, said yes more often than no, and came out more capable, more confident, and often more fulfilled.

A few quick tips if you're looking to grow:

Get Clear on What You Want – What does "growth" mean to you? How do you define success in this stage of your career journey?

Say Yes to Something That Feels Like a Stretch – That project, rotation, or cross-functional task force might be your next leap.

Talk to People – Ask leaders what helped them grow. Ask peers what they see in you.

Stay Bendy – Be open to paths you didn't plan for.

You don't have to have it all figured out. Just be intentional. Stay open. And keep growing.

INSIGHT #19 – MENTORSHIP: ONE ASK AWAY

Want to ask someone to be your mentor, but feel awkward bringing it up? Here's how I have approached it.

Start with clarity. Before reaching out to anyone, know what you want to work on. Are you trying to grow as a people leader? Navigate a career pivot? Build influence in your role? Know your goals!

Mentorship is most impactful when you can say:

"Here's where I am. Here's where I'm trying to go."

Once you know that, reach out with a clear, respectful ask. Here are a few practical phrases that work:

- *"I really admire the way you've led your team through tough changes. I'm working on becoming a more adaptive and resilient leader. Would you be open to being a mentor to me as I grow in this area?"*
- *"I'm trying to sharpen my business acumen and think more strategically. Would you consider mentoring me over the next few months as I work on this?"*
- *"Your journey is exactly how I hope to grow. Would you be open to a short-term mentorship? I'd love to learn from you directly."*

Be direct, be kind, and keep the pressure low. Most people won't be offended by being asked to mentor. They will be honored.

If they say no, it's okay. Don't take it personally. People say no for countless reasons, most of which have nothing to do with you. The reason is most likely timing, capacity, or priorities. It's not rejection, it's redirection.

So, ask. Be brave. Be specific. You never know where a single conversation might lead.

42

LEADERSHIP AND MANAGEMENT SKILLS

Leadership is a skillset, not a title. This section focuses on the practical tools leaders need to build trust, drive clarity, and help their teams thrive.

INSIGHT #20 – COACHING VS. MANAGING: KNOWING WHEN TO SHIFT GEARS

This is a big one for new people leaders. Honestly, I have seen some seasoned leaders who may not have fully learned this yet. Being a people leader means knowing when to guide and when to decide. I can't emphasize this enough.

The best leaders don't live in just one mode. They shift intentionally between coaching and managing. Expert-level leaders make this look effortless, like your favorite NASCAR driver on their favorite track.

Let's break it down.

- *Managing is about direction, clarity, and accountability.*
- *Coaching is about curiosity, development, and empowerment.*

Here's where it gets powerful: the magic happens when you know when to switch.

- **Example 1**: A new team member is unsure of a process. This is a moment to manage. Provide structure. Share the "how" and the "why." Build their confidence by giving them a firm foundation.
- **Example 2**: A seasoned employee brings you a challenge. Coach. Ask open-ended questions. Invite reflection. Let them stretch. You're not there to fix it, you're there to help them grow through it.
- **Example 3**: There's a tight deadline and zero room for error. Manage. Lead decisively. Prioritize speed and execution. You can circle back and coach later, once the fire drill is over.

- **Example 4**: A team member is stuck in self-doubt.
  Coach. This is where trust and belief matter most.
  Help them see what you see. Ask, don't tell.

Great leaders switch between these roles fluidly, based on what their people need in the moment. And getting it wrong can have consequences. If you manage when you should coach it can feel like micromanagement. When you coach when the answer really doesn't lie within them you can cause frustration.

The goal isn't to be one or the other. It's to know the difference and move with intention and empathy.

INSIGHT #21 - THE BEST MANAGERS KNOW THIS SECRET: DELEGATE TO ELEVATE

One of the biggest mindset shifts a manager can make is this: Delegation is not about giving up control. It is about unlocking potential. You can't do it all, and you shouldn't try.

Too many leaders hesitate. "It's easier if I just do it myself," or "I don't want to burden my team." But when you hold onto everything, you're not just limiting your own impact - you're holding back your team's growth.

Great managers delegate with intention. They:

- ☑ Empower team members with meaningful challenges
- ☑ Build confidence and capability
- ☑ Free up time for high-impact work

But here's the key: not all tasks are created equal. The best ones to delegate are those that:

- Align with someone's career goals
- Stretch their skills or expose them to new stakeholders
- Offer visibility or leadership opportunities

Delegation isn't dumping. Delegation is intentional. Dumping is reactive. Dumping looks like offloading tasks without context, clarity, or connection to development. It feels transactional. Delegating is strategic. It's about matching the right task to the right person, with the right support. It's a development tool, not a to-do list transfer.

If you're a leader, ask yourself: What's one task you're holding onto that someone else could own and grow from? Try delegating it this week. You might be surprised at what your team (and you) can achieve.

47

INSIGHT #22 – ARE YOU SETTING THE DIRECTION FOR YOUR TEAM OR JUST REACTING TO THE WINDS OF CHANGE?

Leaders, it's time to face the question: Are you steering the ship or is the ship steering you?

Every team deserves a leader with a clear vision and strategy. A roadmap for where they're going and how they'll get there. Without it, teams drift. Motivation wanes. Priorities blur. And when the inevitable challenges come, your team will struggle to navigate because they're unclear about the destination.

When you dive into a new year (fiscal or calendar), here's the challenge: Step up. Set the direction.

Being a leader isn't just about solving problems or managing the day-to-day. It's about proactively designing the future for your team. It's about looking at the year ahead, asking the hard questions, and aligning on a strategy that drives results and inspires action.

Here's the reality:

A team without a strategy doesn't grow, it stagnates.

A team without clarity on direction doesn't innovate, it hesitates.

A team without a leader who prioritizes vision becomes just a group of individuals checking boxes.

The best leaders are architects of progress. They commit to defining what success looks like, not just for the organization but for their people. They ensure every team member knows the "why" behind their work and how their contributions fit into the bigger picture. They ensure success is properly defined and communicated using a shared language.

Ask yourself these questions:

- *Have I mapped out my team's priorities for the year?*
- *Can my team articulate the vision as clearly as I can?*
- *Am I leading with purpose or simply reacting to what's thrown my way?*

If your answer is no to any of these questions, here's how you can course correct:

- **Reset the Vision -** Take time to clarify and document your team's strategic priorities. Share them in a way that's simple, memorable, and repeatable. Make sure your team knows not just what they're doing, but why it matters.

- **Create a Shared Narrative -** Vision is not just a statement, it is a story. Help your team see how their work fits into the broader journey. Use consistent language and metaphors to reinforce direction and purpose.
- **Communicate with Intention -** Don't wait for the perfect moment. Use team meetings, 1:1s, and informal check-ins to reinforce the vision. Invite your team to reflect on how their work aligns with it. Make it a living conversation.
- **Build Confidence Through Clarity -** People follow leaders who know where they are going. Leading with clarity and conviction gives your team the confidence to move forward even in uncertainty.

This is your opportunity to rise to the occasion. Lead boldly. Be intentional. And most importantly, give your team the confidence that they're following someone who knows where they're going.

INSIGHT #23 - BEFORE THE FLAMEOUT: SPOT THE SPARK OF BURNOUT

Have you ever noticed that subtle dip in energy or that quiet shift in someone's behavior that tells you something is off? Burnout rarely shows up all at once. It starts with small, easy-to-miss signals that leaders often overlook.

Early signs can look like this:

- Someone who is normally upbeat becomes short or easily irritated.
- A high performer starts missing small details or double-checking work they used to breeze through.
- A team member who used to volunteer ideas pulls back and stays quiet in meetings.
- The person who once showed genuine enthusiasm now sounds flat, tired, or disengaged.
- Work that once energized them now feels like a chore.

These are not just signs of exhaustion. They are invitations for leaders to step in with curiosity and care.

Here are a few tips to energize your team and keep burnout at bay:

- **Open the Lines of Communication** – Regular one-on-ones aren't just check-ins; they're opportunities to genuinely connect. Ask your team how they're doing beyond the tasks at hand. Sometimes, all it takes is a heartfelt conversation to uncover underlying stress. During times of stress this takes real intention.

- **Champion Work-Life Balance** – Encourage breaks, flexible hours, or even a digital detox day. When your team sees that you value well-being over endless hustle, they're more likely to recharge and come back with fresh ideas and renewed energy.
- **Celebrate Every Win** – Big or small, victories matter. Recognizing achievements not only boosts morale but also reinforces the message that every effort counts. A simple acknowledgment can transform a challenging day into a steppingstone toward growth.
- **Invest in Their Growth** – Offer opportunities for professional development and skill-building. When your team feels that their career journey matters, they're more engaged, motivated, and less likely to feel trapped in the day-to-day grind.

Remember, leadership isn't just about driving results, it's about cultivating an environment where people can thrive. By spotting burnout early and taking proactive steps, we create a culture that not only endures challenges but also celebrates every step of the journey.

Let's lead with empathy and ensure that our teams are energized, empowered, and ready to conquer any obstacle.

INSIGHT #24 - THE SECRET TO MOTIVATING YOUR TEAM? IT'S NOT WHAT YOU THINK

I've always admired leaders who really know their people. The ones who understand what makes each person light up and don't assume everyone is motivated the same way. My best leaders did this for me, and I've tried to bring that same intention to my own teams.

Real motivation isn't about pushing people to work harder. It's about tapping into what inspires them to want to give their best. When you find what truly excites someone, everything changes.

The strongest teams aren't powered by micromanagement, endless meetings, or pressure. They thrive on purpose, recognition, and trust.

Here's how you can inspire your team to bring their best every day:

Connect to Purpose – People want to know their work matters. Show them how their contributions make a real impact on customers, the company, and the team's success.

Recognize Often – A simple "thank you" or public recognition (for those who appreciate public displays) can ignite motivation like nothing else. Catch people doing great work and celebrate them!

Give Ownership – No one likes to be told exactly how to do their job. Empower your team to take ownership of their work, make decisions, and bring creative solutions.

Lead with Optimism – Energy is contagious. Bring enthusiasm, positivity, and belief in your team's potential. People will rise to the expectations you set.

Motivation isn't about quick fixes; it's about creating an environment where people feel valued, inspired, and ready to go the extra mile.

INSIGHT #25 – BECOMING AN EMPATHETIC LEADER: A JOURNEY WORTH TAKING

In leadership, it's easy to get swept up in metrics, milestones, and meetings. But leadership isn't only about driving results. It's about elevating people. Take a moment and ask yourself: When was the last time you truly saw the people around you? Not just as roles or responsibilities, but as human beings with goals, doubts, and lives far beyond the walls of work.

Empathy isn't a soft skill. It's a strategic advantage. It's the difference between managing tasks and inspiring transformation. When leaders lead with empathy, they unlock trust, foster psychological safety, and create cultures where people feel seen, heard, and valued.

Empathetic leadership starts with intentional presence. Here's how to begin:

- **Listen to Understand - Not to Reply** – Put down the phone, close the laptop, and give someone your full attention. Listening is one of the most generous acts of leadership.
- **Ask Deeper Questions** – Move beyond "How are you?" to "What's bringing you energy lately?" or "What's been weighing on you?" These questions open doors to real connection.
- **Acknowledge Emotions** – You don't need to fix everything. But you do need to notice. A simple "That sounds really tough" can be more powerful than a dozen solutions.

- **Create Space for Vulnerability** – Empathy thrives where people feel safe to be imperfect. Model that safety by sharing your own challenges and learning moments.
- **Act with Consistency** – Empathy isn't a one-time gesture, it's daily practice. It shows up in how you give feedback, how you handle mistakes, and how you celebrate wins.

When leaders lead with empathy, teams become more resilient, more engaged, and more innovative. People take risks, speak up, and stretch themselves because they know they're supported. As you grow in empathy, you grow as a leader. You become more grounded, more self-aware, and more capable of navigating complexity with clarity and compassion.

Empathy doesn't require perfection or even agreement. It requires presence. It's not about having all the answers. It's about showing up for people with curiosity, humility, and heart.

Becoming an empathetic leader is a journey. But it's one worth taking, because it transforms not just your leadership, but your legacy.

INSIGHT #26 – LEADERS, IT'S TIME TO BUILD YOUR BENCH!

If you're not actively building a pipeline of future talent, you're letting down your team, your organization, and yourself.

Leadership isn't just about hitting this quarter's goals or executing today's strategies. It's about setting your team up for sustained success, even when you're no longer in the room or the role. That means investing in the future.

Ask yourself:

- *Who is ready to step into greater responsibility?*
- *How am I actively mentoring and developing emerging talent?*
- *What am I doing to connect with potential future internal or external talent that can thrive on my team?*

- *What am I doing to ensure the next generation of leaders is stronger than the last?*

Great leaders don't just hire for the moment; they cultivate for the future. They identify potential, nurture growth, and equip their team members with the skills and confidence to take the reins when the time comes.

Building a talent pipeline requires intentionality:

Spot the Spark – Pay attention to those who show curiosity, resilience, and initiative, even and especially if they don't have all the answers.

Provide Stretch Opportunities – Assign projects that challenge people to grow outside their comfort zones.

Share What You Know – Mentor, coach, and be transparent about what it takes to lead.

Create a Legacy – Leadership isn't a position; it's an impact.

Identify one person you can intentionally invest in. Start small. A conversation with someone interested in your work, a new responsibility for a team member, or even sharing feedback that somebody can use to grow.

The leaders of tomorrow are in your sphere today. Are you doing your part to prepare them? Or are you leaving their potential and your legacy to chance?

INSIGHT #27 – ARE YOUR ONE-ON-ONE'S DRIVING PERFORMANCE OR JUST GOING THROUGH THE MOTIONS?

Let's talk about an underutilized tool in leadership: the one-on-one meeting.

Too often, these conversations become nothing more than status updates or problem-solving sessions. You check a box, discuss tasks, and move on. If your one-on-ones aren't driving engagement, development, and alignment, you might be missing the point.

People don't need another meeting. They need a leader who listens, challenges, and empowers them to succeed.

The most productive one-on-ones focus on:

✓ **Development** – What skills are they building? What's getting in their way? How can you support their growth?

✓ **Alignment** – Are they clear on priorities? Do they understand how their work connects to the bigger picture?

✓ **Engagement** – What motivates them? How can you remove barriers to their success?

✓ **Recognition** – What are they doing well, and how are you celebrating it?

These meetings should be about them. Their growth. Their aspirations. Their experience at work. Your job is to guide the conversation and then listen more than you talk.

In your next one-on-one:

- *Stop making it a task update.*
- *Start having real conversations that drive growth.*

Leave your team feeling seen, heard, and ready to act. Are you ready to make your one-on-one's count? Step up and lead better conversations this year.

INSIGHT #28 – IF YOUR STAKEHOLDERS DON'T TRUST YOU, THEY WON'T BACK YOU

Leaders, are you truly building trust with your stakeholders or just assuming they're on board?

Influence is earned through relationships, not assumptions. You can have the smartest strategy in the room, but execution will stall if the people around you don't understand your direction or trust the way you lead. Work doesn't move forward in isolation. When stakeholders feel surprised, left out, or unclear, they push back, slow down, or quietly disengage.

Stop assuming. Start communicating with intention.

Building trust with stakeholders means:

- **Clarity** – Do they know what you're doing, why you're doing it, and how it impacts them?
- **Consistency** – Are you keeping people informed before they have to chase you for answers?
- **Collaboration** – Are you involving them early enough to shape the work, or only looping them in at the end to rubber-stamp decisions?
- **Credibility** – Do you deliver on what you commit to, own your results, and show reliability in the moments that matter?

Stakeholder trust isn't built in a single meeting. It accumulates through every update, every expectation you set, and every follow-through that proves you mean what you say.

So, ask yourself:

- *Do my stakeholders trust my leadership?*
- *Am I communicating proactively, or just when there's a problem?*
- *Am I making it easy for them to support and champion my work?*

62

Leadership is not only about leading teams. It is about leading relationships at every level of the organization.

Who do you need to inform, re-engage, or rebuild trust with today?

INSIGHT #29 - WE WERE ALL CREATIVE ONCE... WHAT HAPPENED?

When we were kids, creativity wasn't a skill we practiced. It was our default setting. A cardboard box became a spaceship. A living room became a stage. A crayon became a tool for imagining entire worlds. We didn't worry about being right. We didn't fear being judged. We created because it felt natural.

Then life got louder. School taught us to follow the rules. Work taught us to prioritize efficiency. Deadlines, structure, and expectations slowly pushed imagination into the background. Before long, creativity became something "extra" instead of something essential.

The creativity we had as kids never disappears. It just gets buried under responsibilities, pressure, and the fear of getting things wrong. And in today's fast-changing world, creativity isn't a luxury. It's a competitive advantage. Teams who think differently, experiment often, and approach challenges with curiosity are the ones who grow, innovate, and adapt.

If you want creativity to thrive on your team, you must create the conditions for it to resurface.

Here are six practical ways to encourage creativity in the workplace:

- **Make Space for Play** - Schedule time for brainstorming without judgment or immediate deliverables. Try "creative warm-ups" like doodling, storytelling, or idea sprints.
- **Encourage Curiosity** - Reward questions, not just answers. Host "What if?" sessions to explore unconventional ideas.
- **Break the Routine** - Change meeting formats or locations. Introduce "no agenda" time for open discussion and exploration.
- **Celebrate Risk-Taking** - Normalize failure as part of the creative process. Share stories of bold ideas, whether they worked or not.
- **Cross-Pollinate Ideas** - Mix teams from different departments for fresh perspectives. Invite guest speakers or run internal "TED-style" talks.

- **Lead by Example** - Leaders should model creative thinking and vulnerability. Share your own creative challenges and how you overcame them.

Creativity isn't lost. It's dormant. And with intention, environment, and encouragement, it wakes back up.

The leaders who reignite creativity in their teams don't just get better ideas. They unlock energy, engagement, and a culture where people feel brave enough to imagine again.

INSIGHT #30 - ACCOUNTABILITY ISN'T MEAN - IT'S MEANINGFUL

Let's talk about one of the most misunderstood and avoided responsibilities of leadership: holding people accountable.

Too many leaders tiptoe around tough conversations. They soften expectations to avoid discomfort. They hope problems will magically fix themselves. They convince themselves that being nice is the same as being supportive. When you avoid accountability, you do not protect people, you limit them. And you undermine the team you are trying to lead.

Accountability is not about being harsh. It is about being honest. It is about showing someone you believe in their potential enough to challenge them. It is about refusing to settle for mediocrity because you know what they are capable of.

High-performing teams are not built on wishful thinking. They are built on courage, clarity, and consistent follow-through.

If you want to get better at holding others accountable, start here:

☑ **Set Clear Expectations** – Ambiguity is the enemy of accountability. Make sure your team knows exactly what's expected of them when it comes to performance, behavior, and mindset.

☑ **Address Issues Early** – Small problems don't fix themselves; they multiply. Have the conversation now, not six months from now.

☑ **Lead with Fairness, Not Fear** – Accountability isn't about punishment, it's about growth. Approach tough conversations with the mindset of helping someone improve, not tearing them down.

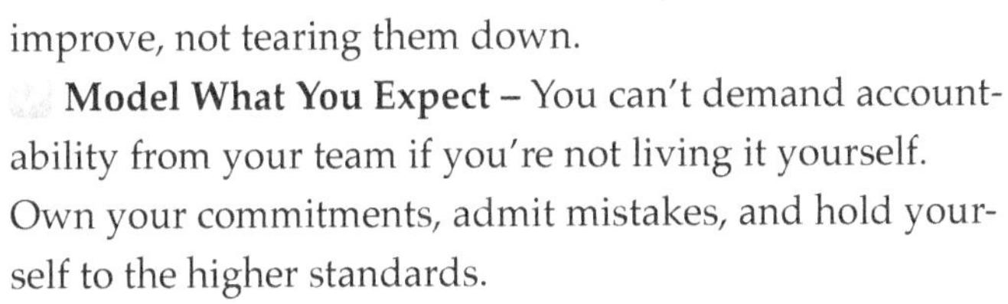 **Model What You Expect** – You can't demand account-ability from your team if you're not living it yourself. Own your commitments, admit mistakes, and hold your-self to the higher standards.

Strong leaders do not avoid accountability, they embrace it. Because they know it is the path to performance, trust, and growth.

Think about one situation you have been avoiding. One person who deserves clarity. One expectation you need to reinforce.

Have the conversation. Reset the standard. Lead with courage and heart. Accountability is not about being tough. It is about caring enough to expect more and helping people rise to it.

INSIGHT #31 – BUSINESS IQ: THE REAL LEADERSHIP EDGE

Do you want to lead strategically? Then you need to understand the business.

If you don't know how your organization makes money, where it's headed, and what risks it faces, you are not truly leading. You are simply managing tasks and processes. Real leadership requires seeing the full picture and making decisions that move the organization forward.

Business and financial acumen are not optional. They are essential for influencing strategy, collaborating across functions, and earning credibility with senior leaders. If you want your voice to matter at the table where decisions are made, you need to speak the language of business.

Stop thinking like a function. Start thinking like a business.

That means:

- **Understanding Financials** - Can you read a profit and loss statement? Do you know what drives revenue, costs, and profitability? Understanding the numbers allows you to make smarter, more informed decisions.
- **Seeing the Bigger Picture** - Can you connect your team's work to the organization's goals and long-term strategy? Every initiative should tie back to the broader mission. Leaders who understand context make better choices.
- **Making Smarter Decisions** - Do you weigh trade-offs, risks, and ROI before advocating for resources or proposing new initiatives? Thinking commercially means making decisions that balance short-term gains with long-term impact.
- **Speaking the Language of Leadership** - Can you frame your ideas in terms of business impact, not just effort? Leaders who translate their work into outcomes, metrics, and value gain trust and influence.

The leaders who rise in organizations are not just great at execution. They think strategically, act commercially, and lead decisively. They understand how their choices affect the entire system, and they influence others to see and act with that same perspective.

Ask yourself:

• *Do I truly understand how my company creates value and for whom?*
• *Am I thinking like a business owner, not just a department leader?*
• *What steps am I taking to strengthen my financial and strategic acumen?*

Sharpening your Business IQ is not just a career advantage. It is the foundation for making confident decisions, leading effectively, and shaping the future of your organization. If you want to lead at the next level, the time to start is now.

INSIGHT #32 – THE PLAYER/COACH MODEL: GREAT INTENT, RISKY REALITY

Are we leaning too hard into the player/coach model of leadership?

With baby boomers retiring and org charts flattening, we're asking leaders to carry increasingly heavier loads. We might be crossing a line.

Younger managers are stepping into bigger shoes. That's great news for growth and opportunity! But more often, I see new leaders being met with an exhaustive list of duties like this:

- Lead the team
- Coach every person
- Deliver outcomes
- Manage change
- Drive culture
- Complete this project
- Oh - and do your actual job too

That is not leadership development. That is a recipe for burnout. It is no wonder that at least once a week, I speak with managers who say they would not choose to manage others if they could start over. Less early career professionals are actively seek leadership roles. They are burning out before they even begin.

Do our leaders really have the time and support they need to lead well? (Hint: it's a rhetorical question.)

So how do we preserve the intent behind the player/coach model while reducing the risk?

- **Clarify Capacity -** Be real about how much time leaders have for coaching and strategy. Adjust expectations accordingly.
- **Coach the Coach** - Provide high-quality development and peer forums where managers can process, vent, and grow.
- **Create Coaching Moments, not Marathons** – Help leaders build coaching into daily touchpoints instead of blocking out hours they don't have.
- **Simplify the Noise** - Give leaders fewer priorities so they can focus on the things that matter. They should focus on people, performance, and purpose.

The best leaders don't do it all. They prioritize what matters most.

Let's not just promote people, we must prepare them. Because the future of leadership isn't just about being in the game. It's about knowing when to lead from the field and when to step back and guide from the sideline.

INSIGHT #33 – LEADERSHIP FEEDBACK ISN'T A TRAP - IT'S A TOOL

Getting meaningful feedback is hard, especially when you are a leader.

One of the biggest mistakes leaders make is assuming silence means everything is fine. Another common one is asking, "What can I do better?" during a one-on-one. Better than nothing, sure, but still too vague to be helpful.

Here is a process I recommend for leaders who genuinely want to get more robust feedback:

Identify – It's important to start with knowing what you want to work on. A key tenant for getting valuable feedback is being specific. Maybe you don't give enough structure, or you dominate meetings, or you are stingy with recognition. We all have something we want to work on.

Advertise (and when needed, Apologize) – Once you know what you want to work on, you must inform others. I know, that may sound scary. No one said being a leader was easy or doesn't require bravery.

I recommend telling your team or key stakeholders. It might go something like this - "Team, I have noticed that sometimes I do X behavior, and I am striving to be better. Here is what I plan to do about it."

Depending on how impactful this behavior has been on people you may even have to apologize for how you have affected others. It levels the playing field and might disarm those who are suspicious of you sharing your challenges more broadly. Remember, a genuine "I'm sorry" will do. Don't explain your behavior away for risk of coming across as excusing or justifying it.

Empower – I have found that for this approach to be effective you must follow up advertising with empowerment. I could look like this "I am going to need help working on X. I don't think I can do this alone. I want to invite you to reach out and give me feedback to help hold me accountable."

I have seen some leaders create a "high sign" the team members can use to help them recognize they are exhibiting that pesky behavior. One of my leaders asked us to tug on our ear if she was getting too direct in meetings.

Follow-up – I get it, you probably feel that this step is obvious. It is important to say it out loud. I have seen this process break down when we don't follow up. You can't ask for help and never talk about it again. Then people will think it was all a show, and you will lose credibility.

Leadership feedback is not a trap. It is a tool. A powerful one. Stop assuming people will speak up on their own. Get intentional, build the structure, and invite the kind of feedback that helps you grow.

Want better feedback? Go first.

INSIGHT #34 – LEADING WITHOUT AUTHORITY? YEAH, IT'S HARD, BUT HERE'S HOW YOU DO IT

Leading without authority can feel like trying to steer a ship without a rudder. You have the vision, the ideas, and the drive. You just don't have the title or the built-in power. I've been there, and you can lead from where you are and make a real impact.

I have watched people influence major decisions and meaningful change without a single direct report. They did it by mastering the quiet power of earned influence. This is the kind of influence that comes from character, competence, and connection. It is built through trust, not titles.

Here are six things that work when you're leading without authority:

- **Get Insanely Clear on Your "Why."** – People follow clarity and conviction. If you don't know why something matters, neither will they. Root your message in purpose, not just process.
- **Lead with Listening** – Want to influence someone? Start by listening to them. Understand their goals, frustrations, and language. Influence starts with empathy.
- **Build Credibility Through Action** – Consistency builds trust. Deliver, follow through, and show up prepared, especially when no one's watching.
- **Communicate with Intention** – Influence isn't about talking more, it's about talking smarter. Speak their

language, tell the story, and connect your ideas to their priorities.

- **Invest in Relationships Before You Need Them –** Don't wait until you need buy-in to build trust. Take interest in people, support their work, and celebrate their wins.
- **Be the Energy You Want to See –** Positivity is magnetic. If you want others to lean in, you must bring the spark. Be curious. Be engaged. Be someone people want to follow.

You don't need a title to make a difference. You need vision, courage, and the willingness to do the hard (but human) work of connection.

INSIGHT #35 - MAKING THE LEAP: FROM INDIVIDUAL CONTRIBUTOR TO LEADER

Moving from individual contributor to leader is one of the biggest and most challenging transitions you'll experience in your career. You're no longer responsible only for your own performance. Now you're accountable for how others perform, grow, and collaborate. It's no longer about checking tasks off your list. It's about empowering a team to deliver results together. This shift isn't just a promotion. It's a true transformation.

The first three months matter more than you think. They set the tone and shape perceptions. They are your opportunity to build trust, establish credibility, and define how you show up as a leader.

Here are a few practical ways to start strong:

- **Learn Before You Lead** – Spend more time listening than talking. Every meeting is situational but aim for a 70/30 ratio: 70% listening and 30% talking. Meet 1:1 with your team. Ask what's working, what's getting in their way, and what they need from you. Their answers will shape your approach and signal that you value their perspective.

- **Shift your Mindset** – You don't need to be the smartest person in the room. You need to create space for others to bring their best ideas forward. Leading is less about doing and more about enabling.

- **Set Clear Expectations Early** – Clarity builds confidence. Define what success looks like for your team and for yourself. Ambiguity is the enemy of trust. So, get specific, especially around communication and decision-making.
- **Build Relationships, Not Just Results** – People don't follow titles, they follow people. Show up with empathy, ask how folks are really doing, and be human. The best leaders lead with both heart and head.
- **Find Your Anchor** – What values or principles will guide your leadership? Define them early. They'll help you navigate the inevitable moments of uncertainty.
- **Get a Mentor. Now.** – Find someone who's already walked this path. Their insight will be gold, especially when the job feels lonely (and sometimes it will).

If you're stepping into leadership for the first time, or mentoring someone who is, remember this: you don't need to have every answer on day one. What you do need is curiosity, humility, and the willingness to grow faster than the role demands. Leadership is not a finish line. It is a practice. The best leaders keep learning, keep listening, and keep choosing to show up even on the days it feels hard.

This transition will stretch you. It will also show you what you're capable of. Step into it with intention. The way you lead now will shape the leader you become next.

INSIGHT #36 – WHEN CHANGE BECOMES TOO MUCH: HOW TO LEAD THROUGH THE FOG

I'll never forget a moment a few years ago when I looked around at my team. They were talented, committed, and usually full of energy. But that day, it was obvious they were running on empty.

It wasn't one big change that did it. It was the pile of them. New priorities. New tools. New org shifts. Every week brought something else, and it was starting to take a real toll.

That's when I learned something important. Change fatigue doesn't mean your team is weak. It means they're human.

And when that fog rolls in, people rarely say "I'm tired." You hear it in the silence. You see it in the dip in creativity. You feel it in the sigh before a meeting or the blank stare after a big announcement.

So how do we lead when the change becomes too much?

Here's what I've learned works, using some of the most reliable practices of effective change leadership:

✓ **Anchor in Purpose** – I made a point to connect every change back to our larger mission and why the work matters. When people understood the purpose behind the chaos, their energy shifted.

✓ **Protect Their Focus** – At one point, we pressed pause on a few initiatives that weren't mission-critical. That one move gave the team space to breathe and showed that their well-being mattered more than our project calendar.

✓ **Communicate More Than Feels Necessary** – When I thought I'd said something enough, I said it again. And then again. Repetition created a feeling of steadiness in the swirl.

✓ **Celebrate What's Steady** – We made a point to shine a light on what wasn't changing. Our values. Our relationships. The things we could still count on.

✓ **Hold Space for Honesty** – We created time just to talk. Not about tasks. About how people were actually doing. Some of those moments became the most meaningful leadership conversations I've ever had.

Leading through change fatigue isn't about having a perfect plan. It's about showing up with empathy, clarity, and care, day after day.

The fog may not lift right away. But when your team knows you're walking through it with them, the path forward gets clearer.

INSIGHT #37 – NAVIGATING TEAM CONFLICT WITHOUT AVOIDANCE: A LEADERSHIP SKILL THAT CHANGES EVERYTHING

Team conflict is inevitable. People with different perspectives, experiences, and working styles will bump into one another. Conflict isn't the problem. Avoiding it is.

When conflict gets ignored, it doesn't disappear. It festers. It shows up in missed deadlines, disengaged teammates, and a whole lot of unspoken tension. Over time, that avoidance erodes trust, morale, and productivity. And when it becomes widespread, it turns into a cultural problem that touches the entire organization.

But handled well? Conflict becomes a catalyst for clarity, collaboration, and even innovation.

Here are seven practical ways to navigate conflict without avoiding it:

Create Space for Healthy Disagreement – In team meetings, normalize phrases like "I see it differently" or "Help me understand your view." Teams thrive when respectful debate is safe and welcomed.

Stay Curious, not Combative – When tensions rise, shift into learning mode. Ask questions like, "Can you share more about what's behind that?" rather than jumping into defense.

Name the Tension Early – Don't wait until it explodes.

A simple "I've noticed some friction - can we talk through it?" can open the door to resolution before things escalate. But, if things heat up don't be afraid to take a break to let cooler heads prevail.

Focus on Shared Goals – Conflict often narrows our vision. Reground the team in what you're collectively trying to achieve, it reminds everyone you're on the same side.

Use "I" Language, not "You" Accusations – "I felt overlooked in that decision" lands very differently than "You left me out." Language matters.

Bring in a Neutral Facilitator When Needed – Sometimes you need an outside perspective to help teams reset. That's not weakness, it's wisdom.

Model It as a Leader – If you avoid tough conversations, your team will too. But if you lean in with respect and courage, you give everyone else permission to do the same.

Conflict can either divide us or deepen our understanding of each other. The difference lies in how we show up. Let's be the leaders who don't dodge the hard moments but turn them into turning points.

INSIGHT #38 - OWNING THE MESSAGE - EVEN WHEN IT'S HARD

One of the toughest parts of leadership is communicating a change you did not initiate and might not fully agree with. You still show up. You still lead. Inside, you wrestle with how to balance authenticity with alignment.

I've been there more than once. Sitting in a meeting thinking, "This is going to land hard, and I am not sure I even believe in it yet." Then walking out and needing to communicate it clearly and confidently to your team. That is leadership in the real world.

Leadership is not about only communicating what excites you. It is about alignment. Your team does not need you to love every decision. They need to trust that you have processed it, internalized it, and can guide them with clarity and confidence. The moment you distance yourself from the message, even subtly, your team feels it. That opens the door to confusion, fear, and disengagement.

Here is how to own the message without losing yourself:

- **Do Your Homework Before You Speak** – Ask questions. Understand the "why" behind the decision. You don't have to agree with everything, but you do need to be able to explain it with context and care.
- **Lead with Empathy, Land with Direction** – Acknowledge that the change might be tough. Then help your team look forward. You could say "I know this is a shift, and it might take some time to adjust.

But here's how we're going to move through it together."

- **Speak in Terms of 'We,' not 'They'** – Saying "they decided…" signals to your team that you are not really in it. Instead, try "we're moving forward with…" or "as a leadership team, we've decided…" These subtle shifts build trust.
- **Separate Emotion from Execution** – It's okay to feel uneasy. But when it's time to communicate, focus on what the team needs to hear to feel informed, grounded, and supported.
- **Make Space Afterward** – After sharing the message, do not just drop it and move on. Invite questions. Be available. People need time to process and often what they need most is simply your presence. Remember that they may be hearing it for the first time. They are going to be in a different place than you.
- **Remember Your Role in the Ripple** – How you deliver the message influences how your team reacts and how they communicate it to others. Own it well, and you create steadiness in the storm.

Leadership is not being a mouthpiece. It is being a bridge. A bridge between the decision and the people who must live with it. A bridge between uncertainty and confidence. A bridge between confusion and clarity.

When you show up with grounded confidence, even when the change is hard, your team can find their footing. That is how leaders turn uncertainty into trust and alignment into action.

Real leadership is not easy. It is essential. It is the difference between teams who flounder and teams who thrive.

INSIGHT #39 – LEADING THROUGH THE UNKNOWN: MICRO HABITS THAT CREATE CLARITY IN CHAOS

I had a tough week that just wasn't going my way. Priorities kept shifting. Decisions were delayed. I was fielding questions I didn't have solid answers for. And still, my team needed direction.

That is the tension of leadership today: being asked to chart a course before the map is even drawn.

Here is what I've learned: your team does not need you to know everything. You may never know all the answers you wish you had. They need clarity in motion. Small, consistent signals that help them focus, act, and feel grounded, even when things feel unsettled.

That is where micro habits come in. These are repeatable leadership behaviors that bring structure to uncertainty. They don't solve the chaos, but they give your team handholds to move forward.

Here are some I rely on:

- **Start each week with a 15-minute clarity scan**. Ask: What is clear? What is uncertain? What is the one thing we can accomplish this week? Then share those insights openly with your team.
- **Use "Even though, we will" language.** For example, "Even though leadership hasn't finalized the plan, we will start drafting the outline by Thursday." This frames uncertainty while maintaining momentum.

- **Narrate your thinking aloud.** Show how you are evaluating options and weighing next steps. It models confident decision-making, even in fluid situations.
- **Anchor to what is steady.** Your values, your purpose, and your customer focus. Naming these points of stability builds trust and psychological safety.
- **End every meeting with one clear next step.** One step forward. No ambiguity. One decision, one task, one owner. Clarity people can act on immediately.

You do not need to eliminate uncertainty to lead effectively. You need to create moments of direction, like mile markers on a winding road. Those moments of clarity are what help teams navigate chaos, maintain confidence, and keep moving forward.

Leadership in uncertainty is not about having all the answers. It is about giving people enough structure, focus, and trust to make the journey together.

INSIGHT #40 – FROM FLASHLIGHT TO FLOODLIGHT: ILLUMINATE DEVELOPMENT GAPS

Trying to figure out why a team doesn't feel supported in their growth and development can feel like pointing a dying flashlight into a dark tunnel. It can be deeply frustrating to see low development and career progression scores in your employee engagement results.

When I sit down with a team or a leader, I don't show up with answers. I show up with questions, because the right questions light the path better than any flashlight ever could.

If you're sensing friction around growth or discontent around development, here is the needs analysis I focus on:

- *Are leaders regularly having meaningful development and career conversations with their people?*
- *What role do they see themselves playing in employee development?*
- *When someone raises their hand with aspirations, how are leaders responding? How well are they equipped to guide those conversations?*
- *Do employees know they own their careers? How have we built the skills and mindsets to help them drive that ownership into the culture?*
- *What growth opportunities realistically exist within the department and what limitations are built into the structure?*
- *What other factors could be at play? Think: compensation, lack of career paths or unclear development expectations.*
- *Can leaders clearly articulate the experiences their people need to grow - either for their current role or future roles?*
- *What does our employee engagement data (or other feedback) tell us?*
- *Could there be team dynamics or elements of culture getting in the way?*

Growth and development are deeply personal and deeply structural. There is no single solution, but slowing down to ask the right questions transforms insight from a weak flashlight beam into a floodlight.

When you see the full landscape clearly, you can identify gaps, remove obstacles, and create development opportunities that move the needle. That is how leaders turn intention into impact.

INSIGHT #41 – THE MYTH OF THE LONE GENIUS (AND WHAT TEAMS REALLY NEED INSTEAD)

Ever hear a leader say, "We just need a rockstar to fix this"? That mindset sounds tempting, but it's a trap. Great teams don't rely on lone geniuses. They rely on people thinking and creating together.

There is a powerful myth in the workplace: that one brilliant mind can crack the code, solve the problem, or spark the next big idea alone. The truth? Innovation rarely happens in a vacuum.

The best ideas come from collaboration across roles, experiences, and perspectives.

When we cling to the lone genius mindset, we:

- *Shut down input*
- *Discourage vulnerability*
- *Create silos*
- *Cause undue pressure*
- *And often… miss the better idea entirely*

Lack of collaboration doesn't just stall creativity. It erodes trust, slows execution, and makes people feel like their voices don't matter.

So how do we move beyond the lone genius myth and build a culture that makes room for real, shared brilliance? The wisdom of the crowd isn't a myth, it is true and even scientifically proven.

Here is how to move from hero to heroes:

☑ **Make Brainstorming a Habit, not a Hero Moment –** Schedule regular, low-stakes opportunities for people to think together, without pressure to have the answer.

☑ **Give Credit Aloud –** When ideas are shared or improved, say the names. It reminds everyone that excellent work is rarely solo work.

☑ **Invite Unexpected Voices –** Ask people outside your function to weigh in. Sometimes the breakthrough comes from the person who is not deep in the weeds.

☑ **Model Collaborative Language –** Use phrases like "building on that idea…" or "what if we tried…" to keep momentum going.

☑ **Reward Generosity –** Recognize not just great ideas but the people who help others shape theirs.

☑ **Normalize Drafts –** Remind your team that draft ideas are welcome. Perfectionism is the enemy of progress.

Create Space to Think – Sometimes the best collaboration happens after people have a chance to reflect. Silence isn't lack of contribution, it's often where insight starts.

The lone genius makes a great story for the big screen, but in real work, breakthroughs happen when we work together and learn from each other. Stop hunting for a hero. Start building the team.

INSIGHT #42 – THE ART OF THE RESET: BOUNCING BACK FROM LEADERSHIP MISSTEPS

No leader gets it right all the time. We say the wrong thing. We act too quickly. We miss the moment that needed more listening.

Leadership is not about perfection. It is about course correction.

The most respected leaders are not the ones who never stumble. They are the ones who know how to reset with humility, courage, and intention. A reset is the moment you choose progress over pride.

So how do you reset when you have taken a wrong turn? Here are powerful ways to rebound, rebuild trust, and refocus your leadership:

- **Name It, Don't Numb It** – Own the misstep. A quick and clear, "I missed the mark on that," goes a long way. Accountability builds credibility.
- **Get Curious, Not Defensive** – Ask for feedback, even when it is uncomfortable. "How did that land for you?" or "What could I have done differently?" opens the door to insight.
- **Model the Messy Middle** – Be transparent with your team as you work through the fix. Show them that growth is not linear and that's okay.
- **Repair the Relationship, Not Just the Outcome** – If trust was damaged, rebuild it one conversation at a time. People do not want perfect leaders. They want human ones.

- **Anchor Back to Values** – Realign your actions with your core leadership values. When you lead from your values, people can feel the shift. It builds authenticity and consistency.
- **Pause to Reflect, Then Move** – Do not rush the reset. Take a beat to learn before jumping back into action. That pause? It's where the growth lives.
- **Stay Future-Focused** – Acknowledge the past, but don't get stuck there. Redirect your energy toward what's next, with clarity and purpose.

Leadership is not about having all the answers. It is about being willing to learn, especially when the lesson is hard.

And if you have taken a wrong step lately, you are not alone. Reset. Recalibrate. Rise. The best leaders do not avoid the fall. They own the rise.

SELF-AWARENESS AND FOUNDATIONAL SKILLS

The work we do starts with who we are. These pieces explore the human side of work and how we manage energy, build resilience, and show up with intention.

INSIGHT #43 – ARE YOU COSPLAYING AS A LEADER? YOUR TEAM CAN TELL

Genuineness is not a "nice to have" in leadership. It is a real advantage.

People can spot a fake a mile away. They may not call it out. They may nod in meetings, smile on Zoom, and say the right things. But they know. And once they sense inauthenticity from a leader, trust quietly begins to erode.

I have seen a lack of genuineness undermine teams full of talent, motivation, and potential. The leader says all the right words, but the energy does not match. The values sound polished, but the behavior feels hollow. Leadership becomes a performance instead of a practice.

That gap is costly. When leaders are "cosplaying" leadership, teams disengage. Innovation slows. Feedback dries up. People stop taking risks and start playing it safe. The culture shifts from ownership to obligation, from commitment to compliance. Not because people do not care, but because they no longer trust what they are being shown.

Genuineness does not mean oversharing or having it all figured out. It means consistency. Integrity. Self-awareness. It means your words and actions line up, even when it is inconvenient. Your values are not proven by what you say in town halls. They are revealed in how you show up on hard days, in tough conversations, and under pressure.

When leaders lead from a place of authenticity, something powerful happens:

- People speak more freely because it feels safe to do so.
- Teams move faster because they are not second-guessing motives.
- Trust deepens because behavior is predictable and values are lived.
- And yes, results improve because energy is spent on the work, not the performance.

So, if you're a leader (or growing into one), ask yourself:

Am I leading from a script instead of from my values?
Where can I be just a little more real, a little more human, today?

Am I leading from the front or by example?

Genuineness is not flashy. It will not win you every room. But it will earn you something far more valuable than applause. It earns trust. *And trust is how leadership lasts.*

INSIGHT #44 - HOW TO OUTRUN PERFECTIONISM AND WIN

Perfectionism feels productive. But it's holding you back.

Let's talk about something I see in so many high performers: perfectionistic thinking.

It shows up like this:

- "I can't share this until it's perfect."
- "What if people think I don't know what I'm doing?"
- "If I get it wrong, I'll lose credibility."

Sound familiar? I've coached brilliant professionals who delay sharing their ideas, raising their hand, or launching something new. It's often not because they're not ready, but because they're afraid it's not flawless.

Perfectionism isn't a standard, it's a shield. A way to protect yourself from criticism, judgment, or failure.

But here's what happens when you let go of perfection:

- You move faster.
- You learn more.
- You grow braver.

You create space for creativity, connection, and experimentation. And that's where real impact lives.

Try this:

- Share your idea with your team and leaders before it's "done."
- Ask for feedback earlier.
- Remind yourself: Done is better than perfect, especially when perfect never comes.

Progress > perfection. Every time. You don't need to be flawless. You need to be engaged.

INSIGHT #45 – THE DOUBLE-EDGED SWORD OF DISCIPLINE AT WORK

Growing up, my dad owned and operated his own Tae Kwon Do studio, so discipline was not an abstract concept in my life. It was practiced daily. I spent years training, repeating forms, refining technique, and learning that progress rarely comes from motivation alone. It comes from showing up, again and again.

That lesson has been a gift in my life. About 90 percent of the time.

Discipline is a superpower in the workplace. It is what helps us meet deadlines when motivation dips, stay focused when distractions are loud, and follow through when the work gets hard. Discipline is the engine behind high performance, personal growth, and long-term success. It is often what separates good intentions from real results.

But like any strength, discipline has a shadow side.

When discipline turns rigid, it stops serving people and starts controlling them. When it becomes the goal instead of the tool, creativity shrinks. Burnout creeps in. Curiosity fades. What once drove excellence can quietly turn into fear, compliance, or exhaustion.

I have seen this play out on teams that prize productivity above all else. The standards are high, but humanity is low. People stop experimenting. They stop speaking up. They do exactly what is asked and nothing more, not because they are lazy, but because the system no longer rewards thinking or risk.

How do we strike the right balance?

✓ **Use discipline as a guide, not a cage.** Structure, routines, and expectations should create clarity and momentum, not suffocation. Discipline should free people to do great work, not trap them in process for process's sake.

✓ **Apply discipline with empathy.** People are not machines. Life happens. Context matters. The leaders who get the most from their teams know when to hold the line and when to flex. Empathy does not lower standards. It makes them sustainable.

✓ **Make sure discipline serves the mission, not ego.** If rules, rituals, or routines exist primarily to maintain control or protect authority, they are likely doing more harm than good. Discipline should point people toward purpose, not obedience.

The healthiest workplaces do not choose between discipline and humanity. They hold both. They expect excellence and make room for people to be human. They value consistency and encourage creativity.

That is when discipline becomes what it was always meant to be. Not a weapon. Not a constraint. But a force for growth, resilience, and lasting success.

INSIGHT #46 – CURIOSITY IS A COMPETITIVE ADVANTAGE

In today's rapidly changing world, one skill consistently stands out as a true game-changer: curiosity.

Curiosity fuels innovation. It drives engagement. It accelerates learning. It helps leaders make better decisions and lead with empathy. And here is the key point many people miss: curiosity is not just a personality trait. It is a skill. One you can strengthen with practice.

When you approach your work and your team with genuine curiosity, you shift how you lead. You move from reacting to exploring. You stop assuming and start asking. You do not just solve problems. You uncover opportunities.

Curiosity also changes the tone of leadership. It replaces certainty with openness. Judgment with interest. Control with learning. In moments of complexity, curiosity creates space for better thinking and stronger collaboration.

How do you build curiosity as a skill? Here are five practical ways:

Ask One More Question – In your next meeting, resist the urge to jump to a solution. Ask, "What else should we consider?" or "What's a perspective we haven't heard yet?" That extra question can spark a breakthrough.
Commit to Continuous Learning – Read broadly. Take in diverse viewpoints. Sign up for that webinar, read that article, or talk to someone outside your usual circle. The

more dots you collect, the more creative your thinking becomes.

Listen to understand, not to reply – Curiosity shows up in how we listen. Slow down. Ask thoughtful follow-up questions. Show that you are invested in understanding, not just responding.

Be Aware of Your Assumptions – Curiosity often gets blocked by certainty. When you feel stuck or frustrated, pause and ask, "What story am I telling myself?" and "Could something else be true?" That's where growth begins.

Create Space for Curiosity on Your Team – Celebrate questions, not just answers. Recognize people for exploring new ideas. Make "I don't know, but let's find out" a safe and celebrated response.

The most effective leaders I know aren't the ones with all the answers. They're the ones who stay curious, especially in complexity.

The next time you're facing a challenge, remember, curiosity doesn't slow you down, it sets you apart. It's not just a mindset. It's your competitive advantage.

INSIGHT #47 – SELF-COACHING THROUGH A TOUGH WEEK

I had a week that was not my best. Deadlines piled up. Some key conversations didn't land the way I'd hoped. I found my mind spinning. I was second-guessing, overthinking, and waking up at three a.m. replaying conversations in my head.

It happens to all of us. No matter how strong your mindset or how developed your leadership skills are, tough times will show up. The key is not avoiding them but learning how to coach yourself through them.

This is where self-coaching becomes a powerful tool.

At its core, self-coaching is the practice of intentionally guiding your thoughts, emotions, and behaviors, much like a great coach would. When you are in the thick of a hard week, this can be the difference between spiraling and finding your footing.

And this matters beyond just you. When one person on a team is quietly struggling, it can subtly shift the tone of meetings, collaboration, and energy. Multiply that across a team or department, and the ripple effects are real.

How do you self-coach when things feel off?

Here are a few techniques that helped:

⬩ **Name the Truth Without Judgment -** Say what is happening. "This week is hard." That is not weakness. It is self-awareness.

⬩ **Ask Better Questions** – Instead of "Why is this

happening to me?" try "What's within my control today?" or "What do I need most right now?"

- ◆ **Zoom Out** – Tough moments feel all-consuming. Remind yourself of the bigger picture. One bad meeting isn't your whole story.
- ◆ **Pick One Win** – Celebrate something. A follow-up email sent. A hard conversation had. A deep breath taken before responding.
- ◆ **Practice Mini Resets** – Walk around the block. Shut your laptop for ten minutes. Resetting your nervous system resets your mindset.
- ◆ **Lean on Your People** – Self-coaching doesn't mean going it alone. Call a trusted friend or colleague. Sometimes just saying things aloud is a release.

Coaching yourself is not about perfection. It is about curiosity, compassion, and clarity, especially when things feel off.

If you are in a tough stretch, keep going. You are not broken. You are building.

INSIGHT #48 - THE TRUST BATTERY: HOW TO RECHARGE AFTER A CREDIBILITY HIT

Ever had someone break your trust at work?

Maybe it was a teammate who promised they would deliver and did not. Or a leader who said they had your back until the pressure was on. It stings. It lingers. And it changes how you show up in ways you do not always realize right away.

And if we are being honest, at some point we have all been on the other side of that equation. Life gets busy. Context gets lost. We drop the ball. We misunderstand. We overpromise with good intentions and underdeliver.

Trust is not built once and put on autopilot. It is charged every day, like a battery. And when that battery drains, it does not recharge on its own. It requires intention, humility, and consistency over time.

Here's how you start building or rebuilding that trust battery:

- **Own Your Missteps Quickly** – Nothing builds more credibility than accountability. Don't deflect. Don't wait. Say: "I missed the mark and here's what I'm doing to fix it." Say "I'm sorry" when necessary and appropriate. Apologies are not a sign of a weakness, but a gesture of respect.
- **Follow Through on the Small Things** – Respond when you say you will. Be on time. Deliver on the unglamorous tasks. These are not just nice to have. They are the daily deposits into your trust account.
- **Understand How They Experienced the Break** – It's not about your intent; it's about their perception. Ask the person you impacted, "How did that affect you?" Listen. No defensiveness. Just curiosity and care.
- **Stack Reliability** – Rebuilding trust isn't a grand gesture, it's a pattern. Consistent, predictable behavior over time signals, "You can count on me."
- **Be Transparent - Especially When Things Are Messy** – Even when you don't have all the answers, communicate openly. Trust builds when people feel informed, not blindsided.
- **Rebuild Relationships Alongside Reputation** – You're not just fixing a mistake, you're restoring a connection. Be human. Be real. Reconnect.

Trust is not a light switch. It is a dimmer. Whether you are building it for the first time or rebuilding after a fall, your credibility grows brighter with every honest interaction. Keep charging that battery. One moment at a time.

INSIGHT #49 – HUMAN SKILLS: THE POWER BEHIND THE WORK

In every industry, across every role, there's a set of skills that quietly powers progress. They're not flashy. They're not technical. But they're essential.

I call them human skills. They are often labeled soft skills, but let's be honest. There is nothing soft about them. In fact, they are some of the hardest skills to learn and master.

These are the skills that make work *work*: the ability to communicate, collaborate, adapt, and lead. Unlike technical skills, which focus on specific tools or knowledge, human skills shape how we apply that knowledge, how we navigate challenges, and how we bring out the best in others.

You can master the latest software, analyze complex data, or engineer the most efficient system. But if you cannot communicate your ideas, collaborate with others, or navigate change, your impact will remain limited.

What sets human skills apart?

They Are Transferable – While technical skills can become outdated, human skills like problem-solving, empathy, and resilience are timeless. They move with you from role to role, industry to industry.

They Drive Innovation – Creativity and adaptability fuel progress, helping organizations evolve in ways that technology alone never could.

They Amplify Technical Expertise – The most effective professionals aren't just knowledgeable, they connect, inspire, and influence. They teach, they translate, and they transfer ideas in ways that stick.

✅ **They Are Contextual** – Human skills flex to fit the moment. Whether you're leading a team through change or navigating a tough conversation, these skills help you read the room, adjust your approach, and respond with intention.

✅ **They Are Relational** – Success rarely happens in isolation. Human skills are what build trust, foster inclusion, and create psychological safety. These are the conditions where people do their best work.

✅ **They Are Durable** - Trends shift. Tools evolve. But the ability to listen, empathize, and communicate with clarity? That never goes out of style.

In a world where AI and automation are reshaping jobs, *human skills are more valuable than ever*. They're what makes people stand out, teams thrive, and businesses succeed.

If you want to boost your impact, invest in your human skills. Because the future of work isn't just about what you do. It's about how you do it.

INSIGHT #50 - RESILIENCE: THE SUPERPOWER FOR A RAPIDLY CHANGING WORLD

Change isn't coming. It's here. New technologies, shifting priorities, reorganizations, and constant demands. It often feels like we're building the plane while flying it.

In that kind of environment, resilience isn't just a nice-to-have. It is essential.

Resilience is what helps you stay grounded when the ground keeps moving. It's the ability to bounce back from setbacks, adapt to change, and keep moving forward with purpose. And it's just as critical for teams as it is for individuals.

What does resilience look like at work?

It looks like:

A team member asking for help instead of hiding a mistake.

A leader staying calm and focused when plans change… again.

A colleague offering encouragement after a tough meeting.

An entire team choosing learning over blame after a project goes sideways.

Resilience isn't about being tough. It's about being adaptable. It's about recovery. And the good news? You can build it.

Here are a few ways to strengthen your own resilience:

- **Normalize Setbacks** – Talk openly about what didn't go as planned and what you learned from it. Growth lives in the debrief conversation.
- **Prioritize Recovery** – Resilience requires rest. Take breaks. Use your time off. Encourage others to recharge, don't just reward burnout.
- **Reconnect to Purpose** – Remind yourself and your team members why the work matters. Purpose fuels perseverance.
- **Practice Flexible Thinking** – When things do not go as expected, shift the focus from "Why is this happening?" to "What's possible now?"
- **Create a Space for Real Talk** – Psychological safety boosts resilience. When people feel safe to speak up, they're more likely to stay engaged and bounce back stronger.

We cannot control the pace of change. But we can control how we show up during it. When we show up with resilience, we give others permission to do the same.

INSIGHT #51 - THE SKILL OF UNLEARNING: LETTING GO TO GROW

In today's fast-paced world, learning gets the spotlight, but unlearning is often the skill that creates growth.

Unlearning often takes more effort than learning because it requires us to release ideas, habits, and ways of working that once served us but no longer do. It's what enables growth.

And in a world, that's evolving faster than ever, the ability to unlearn is what keeps us relevant, resilient, and ready for what's next.

Think about it:

- A leader who always relied on authority must unlearn command-and-control if they want to build psychological safety.
- A top performer who used to do everything solo must unlearn the lone-wolf mindset to thrive in collaborative, team-based environments.
- An expert who was taught "never show uncertainty" might need to unlearn perfectionism to embrace curiosity and growth.

Unlearning isn't about forgetting. It's about choosing to replace outdated thinking with new insight.

Here are some ways to build this powerful skill:

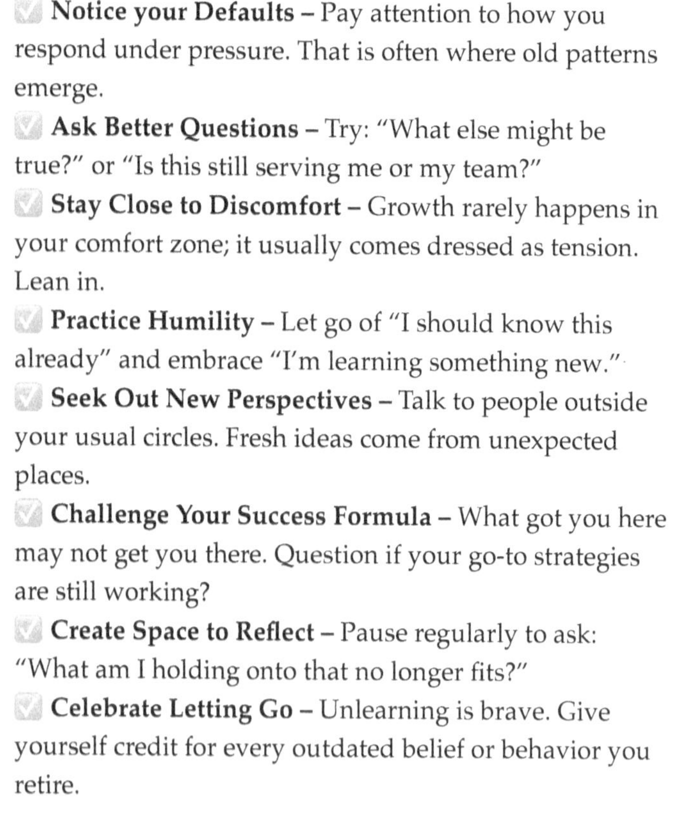

☑ **Notice your Defaults** – Pay attention to how you respond under pressure. That is often where old patterns emerge.

☑ **Ask Better Questions** – Try: "What else might be true?" or "Is this still serving me or my team?"

☑ **Stay Close to Discomfort** – Growth rarely happens in your comfort zone; it usually comes dressed as tension. Lean in.

☑ **Practice Humility** – Let go of "I should know this already" and embrace "I'm learning something new."

☑ **Seek Out New Perspectives** – Talk to people outside your usual circles. Fresh ideas come from unexpected places.

☑ **Challenge Your Success Formula** – What got you here may not get you there. Question if your go-to strategies are still working?

☑ **Create Space to Reflect** – Pause regularly to ask: "What am I holding onto that no longer fits?"

☑ **Celebrate Letting Go** – Unlearning is brave. Give yourself credit for every outdated belief or behavior you retire.

Unlearning is the doorway to growth. If we want to lead in the future, we can't rely on what we have done in the past.

INSIGHT #52 - SLOW DOWN TO SPEED UP

One Saturday, my wife, who will be the first to tell you she is not a morning person, decided to drive herself to a fitness class. I tagged along for support and to check out the new fancy gym.

We pulled into the first gym only to realize it was the wrong location. Or so we thought. We zipped to another location across town. Also, wrong.

Finally, after checking the schedule (which, to be clear, was available the entire time), we returned to the first gym and just in time for her to barely make the class. She nailed it in the end, but it was a chaotic start that could've been avoided with thirty seconds of clarity.

And that's when it hit me: this is exactly what happens at work when we don't slow down.

At work, how many times have we:

- Delivered a project that wasn't aligned to actual needs
- Made decisions before understanding the real problem
- Moved forward on something only to find out we didn't have all the tools and resources we needed.

We live in a fast-paced world. Slowing down isn't laziness, it's leadership. When we pause to ask the right questions, dig into real needs, and create a thoughtful plan, we accelerate impact. We reduce rework, build trust, and deliver results that stick.

Ask before acting. Align before designing. Plan before launching. Slowing down might feel like a delay but it's often the fastest route to success.

Today, let's choose intention over instinct. Clarity over chaos. And maybe... coffee before cardio.

INSIGHT #53 – HEALING FROM WORKPLACE TRAUMA: TURNING PAIN INTO POWER

Work is supposed to be a place where we grow, contribute, and feel a sense of purpose. But for many people, work becomes the place where confidence is shaken, trust is broken, and energy slowly drains away. Toxic leadership. Unrealistic demands. Moments where you felt unseen, unheard, unwelcome, or even betrayed. Those experiences leave a mark.

Even using the phrase workplace trauma can make organizations uncomfortable. It feels heavy. Too emotional. Too personal. But avoiding the language does not erase the impact. It just pushes it underground, where it shows up later as disengagement, burnout, silence, or people quietly opting out.

I have been fortunate to work for some truly incredible leaders. Leaders who challenged me, believed in me, and helped me grow in ways I still carry with me today. And I have also worked for leaders who taught me something just as important. They showed me what not to do. How small moments of carelessness, ego, or unchecked pressure can leave lasting harm. Those experiences shaped my leadership just as much, because they clarified the kind of leader I never want to be.

Workplace trauma is real. And it does not always announce itself loudly. Sometimes it shows up as hesitation to speak up. Sometimes overworking to prove worth. Sometimes as playing small to avoid being hurt again. Left unaddressed, it can follow us from role to role, shaping decisions we do not even realize we are making.

But here is the part that matters most. What happened to you does not get to decide what happens next. Healing is possible. And healing can turn pain into power.

How do we begin to heal?

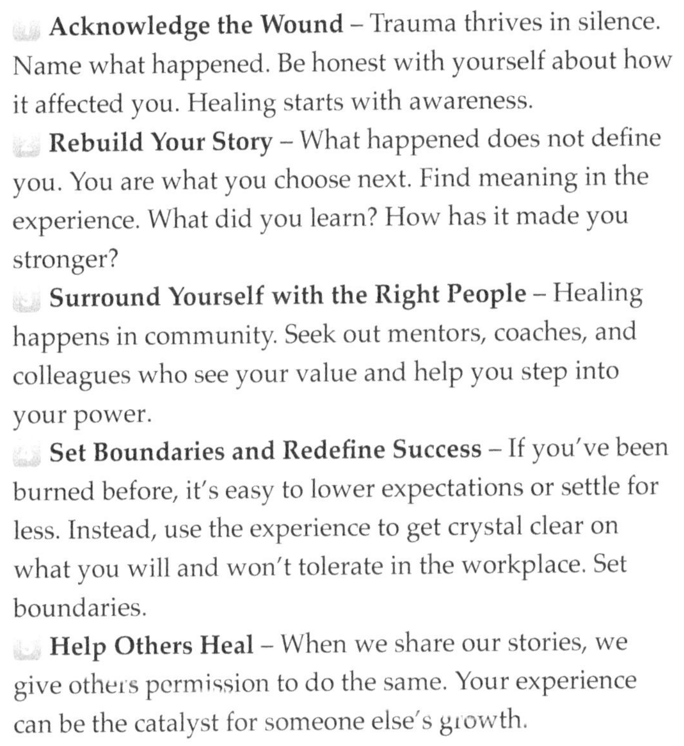

Acknowledge the Wound – Trauma thrives in silence. Name what happened. Be honest with yourself about how it affected you. Healing starts with awareness.

Rebuild Your Story – What happened does not define you. You are what you choose next. Find meaning in the experience. What did you learn? How has it made you stronger?

Surround Yourself with the Right People – Healing happens in community. Seek out mentors, coaches, and colleagues who see your value and help you step into your power.

Set Boundaries and Redefine Success – If you've been burned before, it's easy to lower expectations or settle for less. Instead, use the experience to get crystal clear on what you will and won't tolerate in the workplace. Set boundaries.

Help Others Heal – When we share our stories, we give others permission to do the same. Your experience can be the catalyst for someone else's growth.

You deserve a career that energizes you, not one that leaves scars. The past may have shaped you, but it does not own you. Whether you are healing from harm or leading others forward, the work matters. Because leadership has the power to wound. And it also has the power to heal.

INSIGHT #54 – PEAK PERFORMANCE ISN'T ABOUT TIME - IT'S ABOUT ENERGY

"You must be a robot."

I hear this all the time. Whether it's after a full day of meetings, a late-night writing session, or a weekend workshop, people often ask how I keep my energy so high. The truth? I'm not a robot (promise). I've just learned the value of managing not just time, but energy. It's a real game-changer.

- Time is finite. We all get twenty-four hours.
- Energy, though? That's renewable. And it's the secret to showing up fully, consistently, and joyfully.

Here's the difference:

Time management is about scheduling.
Energy management is about sustainability.

You can have every minute scheduled and still feel exhausted. But when you manage your energy instead of just your time, you create space to do what matters most with clarity, presence, and purpose.

Here are five practical ways I manage my energy (and how you can too):

Start with your body, not your to-do list.

Movement, Hydration, Eating and Sleep are Non-

Negotiables – I treat them like meetings with my future self.

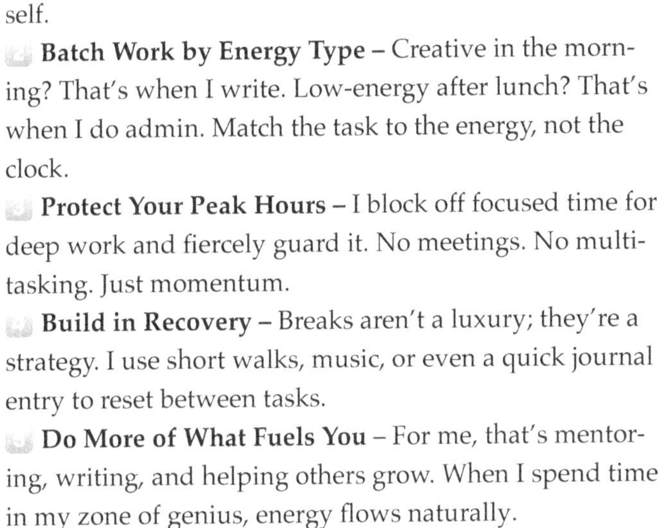 **Batch Work by Energy Type** – Creative in the morning? That's when I write. Low-energy after lunch? That's when I do admin. Match the task to the energy, not the clock.

Protect Your Peak Hours – I block off focused time for deep work and fiercely guard it. No meetings. No multitasking. Just momentum.

Build in Recovery – Breaks aren't a luxury; they're a strategy. I use short walks, music, or even a quick journal entry to reset between tasks.

Do More of What Fuels You – For me, that's mentoring, writing, and helping others grow. When I spend time in my zone of genius, energy flows naturally.

If you've been feeling stretched thin, try shifting the question from "How can I fit this in?" to "How can I show up with energy for what matters most?"

When you manage your energy, you don't just get more done. You do it with heart.

INSIGHT #55 – RESPOND, DON'T REACT: THE SKILL THAT CHANGES EVERYTHING

The email hit me like a punch. You know the kind. It questions your team's work, CCs half the organization, and lands in your inbox at 4:57 PM. I could feel the heat rising in my chest. My first instinct was to fire back, defend, correct, and set the record straight.

But I've learned something the hard way. Leadership lives in the space between the trigger and the response.

Emotional agility is not about ignoring your feelings. It is about pausing long enough to choose how you show up. Taking a breath. Letting the surge pass. That pause is where credibility is built or broken.

In emotionally charged moments at work, tense meetings, tough feedback, unexpected decisions, how you handle yourself matters more than the words you choose. Reactivity may feel justified in the moment, but it often creates cleanup work you never intended.

Here's what's helped me (and many individuals I coach) become more emotionally agile:

- **Notice Without Judgment** – Instead of saying "I shouldn't feel angry," say "I am feeling angry." Naming the emotion is the first step in not being ruled by it.
- **Create Space** – Buy yourself time. Take a walk. Write the email but don't send it. Say, "That's a big topic, can

I get back to you this afternoon?" The pause is powerful.

- **Ask, 'What's My Purpose Here?'** – Will reacting help you move the work or relationship forward? Usually not. Responding with intention keeps the long game in view.
- **Don't Confuse Emotion with Urgency** – Just because something feels urgent doesn't mean it is. Slow down. Most things can wait thirty minutes and the version of you that responds after a reset is a better one.
- **Lead by Example** – When others around you see you staying steady, asking thoughtful questions, or responding with calm clarity, it gives them permission to do the same.

Emotional agility doesn't mean suppressing emotions. It means working with them, not for them.

If you're serious about performing well, don't just manage your calendar, manage your reactions. That's where real influence begins.

INSIGHT #56 – THE POWER OF THE PAUSE: HOW TO RESET IN HIGH-STRESS MOMENTS

It is amazing what a single breath can do.

In the middle of chaos, tight deadlines, tense conversations, and unexpected curveballs, our instinct is to push through. React quickly. Say something. Do something. Keep going.

But what if the most powerful thing you could do is… pause?

Pausing does not mean doing nothing. It means creating a moment to reset. To respond instead of reacting. To regain clarity and composure in the middle of pressure.

High-stress moments are inevitable. But staying stuck in stress? That is optional.

Here are a few ways to pause with intention, especially when the stakes are high:

- **Name What You're Feeling** – Stress clouds our thinking. Saying, "I'm feeling overwhelmed" helps ground you and reduce its intensity.
- **Take a Breath – Literally** – Inhale for four counts, hold for four, exhale for four. (It's called box breathing, and it's proven to help reset your nervous system.)
- **Use a Reset Phrase** – "I've got time to get this right." "Let's get curious, not furious." A short mantra can change your mind set in seconds.
- **Step Away Briefly** – A two-minute walk, a quick stretch, or even standing up can shift your mental state and help you re-engage with more clarity.
- **Ask a Question** – "What's the most important thing

right now?" A simple question creates focus and gives your brain a target when things feel out of control.

 Visualize Success – Imagine the best-case outcome. This helps shift your mind from survival mode into possibility mode.

 Turn the Pause Into a Team Norm – Start meetings with a deep breath or a short grounding moment. You will be amazed how much sharper and kinder the conversation becomes.

The pause isn't weakness. It's wisdom. It is how you stay steady in the storm, and how you lead others through it too. Let's normalize the power of the pause so we can refocus on how to best move forward.

INSIGHT #57 – THE CONFIDENCE-COMPETENCE LOOP: FUELING REAL GROWTH

Ever notice how the more competent you become at something, the more confident you feel? And how that confidence makes you more willing to try, stretch, and grow? That's the confidence-competence loop in action.

Here is how it works:

When you act (even imperfectly), you build skill.

- That skill leads to small wins and progress.
- Progress builds confidence.
- Confidence makes you take more action.

And the loop continues and momentum builds, growth happens.

Most people wait to feel confident before they act. And that is where they get stuck. If you want to grow, you must flip the switch and act before you are ready.

Here are six ways to jumpstart the confidence-competence loop:

Take Messy Action – Stop waiting for perfect conditions. Start with what you know and improve as you go. Confidence is built in the doing.

Track Your Progress – Keep a "small wins" list. It's easy to miss how far you've come. Reflection builds belief in yourself.

Ask More Questions – Curiosity fast-tracks competence. Every question you ask is a step forward in skill and confidence.

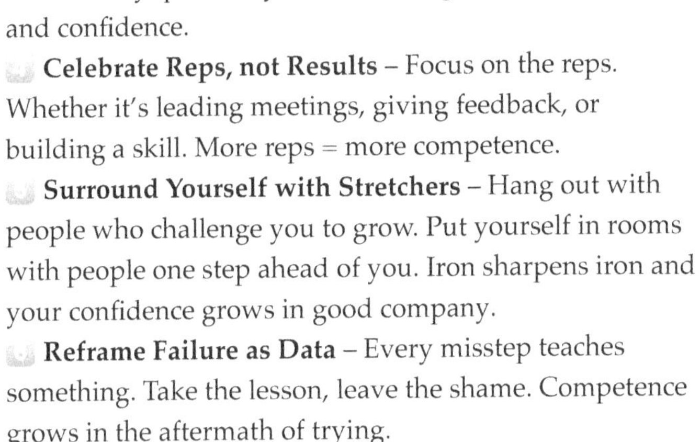 **Celebrate Reps, not Results** – Focus on the reps. Whether it's leading meetings, giving feedback, or building a skill. More reps = more competence.

Surround Yourself with Stretchers – Hang out with people who challenge you to grow. Put yourself in rooms with people one step ahead of you. Iron sharpens iron and your confidence grows in good company.

Reframe Failure as Data – Every misstep teaches something. Take the lesson, leave the shame. Competence grows in the aftermath of trying.

Confidence isn't the starting line. Action is. If you are stuck, start small. One step. One stretch. One rep. Simply move forward.

You don't need to feel ready. You just need to begin.

INSIGHT #58 – THE WORK NO ONE SEES (BUT EVERYONE FEELS)

Let's talk about the invisible workload. You know it. You feel it. It's not on your to-do list, but it's always on your mind.

The mental load is the behind-the-scenes effort of keeping projects, teams, and people moving forward. It's remembering every birthday on the team, tracking status updates in your head, thinking five steps ahead in meetings, or mentally prepping a Plan B for your Plan A… just in case.

It's the emotional and cognitive weight of work that rarely shows up in job descriptions but absolutely impacts performance, stress, and burnout.

Many people carry this invisible load alone. And we do not talk about it enough. Let's change that.

Here are six practical ways to ease the mental load at work, for us and for others:

- **Normalize Asking, "What's on Your Mind?"** – Check in on more than just tasks. Surface the hidden work that might be causing stress or overload.
- **Make Team Knowledge Visible** – Create shared calendars, checklists, and status boards so no one has to keep it all in their head.
- **Rotate Recurring Responsibilities** – Don't let the same person always be the "meeting note taker," "birthday planner," or "emotional glue" of the team.
- **Say No Without Guilt** – Mental load thrives in silence.

Saying no when you are at capacity makes room for honest, healthy conversations.

- **Acknowledge Invisible Effort** – Recognize the emotional labor of mentoring, listening, and supporting others. Do this just like you would a big deliverable.
- **Set "Think Time" Boundaries** – Block calendar time for strategy, reflection, or even just breathing room. Mental work is real work.

We cannot eliminate the mental load, but we can share it more fairly and talk about it more openly.

If you're someone who carries a lot of invisible work… I see you. You are not alone. And it's okay to ask for support.

Let's build teams where all the work, not just what is visible, is valued.

INSIGHT #59 – STRATEGY ISN'T A SECRET CLUB

Over the past few years, I've worked with hundreds of leaders who want to elevate their thinking, expand their influence, and make smarter decisions. One teammate, in particular, stands out. She was eager to grow her strategic muscle but wasn't always sure how to do that in practice.

Through a series of projects, I encouraged her to zoom out, ask sharper questions, and connect her work to the broader business context. We built in regular moments of reflection: What's working? What's not? Where can you stretch your thinking?

Recently, I watched her lead a meeting with our leadership team. She confidently framed the conversation, connected dots across multiple initiatives, and helped the group see the strategic implications of their decisions. It was a full-circle moment and a powerful reminder that when we intentionally create space for people to grow, they do.

Here's what I've seen help leaders grow their strategic thinking:

Zoom Out

Strategic thinkers don't just react, they pause and ask:

- "What's really going on here?"
- "How does this connect to the bigger picture?"

The more you practice pausing to ask reflective questions, the more you'll shift from problem-solving to pattern-spotting.

Connect the Dots

Look at the whole, not just the parts. Notice how your work impacts other teams, functions, and outcomes. Strategy lives in connections, not silos. Learn the business. Ask thoughtful questions. Be curious beyond your role.

Play the Long Game

Tactical thinkers ask, "How can I fix this today?" Strategic thinkers ask, "How can I prevent this from continuing to happen in the future?" Start thinking in terms of weeks, quarters, and years, not just hours and days.

Speak the Language of Impact

Want to sound more strategic? Talk about business outcomes, rather than activity. "I led a training" becomes: "We reduced onboarding time by 30% through a redesigned training experience." Big difference.

Strategic thinking isn't reserved for a select few, and it's not something you're born with. It's a skill you build over time, through intention, reflection, and learning.

If you're ready to shift from doing to driving and from reacting to leading, start now. Strategy isn't a secret club. There's room for you.

INSIGHT #60 – HYBRID WORK: BECAUSE SOMETIMES YOU NEED A CAT'S-EYE VIEW

Sometimes, success is all about shifting your perspective. My cat, Zooey, is a master at this, she never looks at anything the same way twice. It's a skill we "hoomans" can learn from, especially as our work environments evolve.

I work in a hybrid setup, and I love the balance it brings: some days in the office, some days at home. It's the flexibility I need, and I see more people discovering what works best for their own preferences and lifestyles.

In conversations with colleagues, I've noticed that adapting to hybrid work isn't always easy. If you're used to the office, moving to remote or hybrid can feel like starting from scratch. That's why I encourage everyone to rethink how they approach their workday. Start owning your calendar and deciding when you want to do certain types of work.

At home, I focus on:

- Deep, focused work
- Developing ideas and strategies
- Project planning
- Administrative tasks
- Meetings with familiar colleagues and project updates

At the office, I prioritize:

- Team meetings
- One-on-ones and networking
- Collaborative sessions on strategy and planning
- Fun and team-building events
- Open calendar time to connect spontaneously with others

The real shift comes from changing not just how you think, but how you work. Be deliberate about where and how you spend your time. Match the environment to the task or experience you want to create. And when you are in the office, prioritize connection, because building relationships is just as important as getting the work done.

It takes time to find your rhythm, and it may never be perfect. But with a little experimentation, you can get closer to your ideal working scenario. It can make life better for you and your furry friends.

FINAL THOUGHTS: KEEP GROWING, KEEP GOING

If you've made it this far, congratulations, not just for finishing a book, but for investing in yourself and your growth. Quick Bites of Insight™ was never meant to be a one-and-done read. It's a companion for your journey, a spark for your next step, and a reminder that leadership and learning are built in the small moments, not just the big ones.

Remember, you don't need to be perfect to make an impact. You just need to show up curious, present, and willing to try. Every insight, story, and practical tip in these pages is an invitation to experiment, reflect, and stretch a little further than you did yesterday.

Leadership is not about having all the answers. It is about showing up with intention, courage, and heart. It is about building trust, creating clarity, and helping others rise alongside you. Whether you are leading a team, influencing without authority, or simply trying to be a better colleague, your willingness to grow is your greatest asset.

So, as you close this book, ask yourself:

- What's one small shift I can make today?
- Who can I encourage or support on their journey?
- How will I keep learning, even when things get messy?

Growth lives in ordinary moments, made extraordinary by your intention. Celebrate your progress, share your wins, and ask for help or feedback along the way. The future of work and leadership needs your perspective, your energy, and your humanity.

Keep showing up. Keep experimenting. Keep raising the bar. Leadership does not wait for perfect conditions. The world is ready for your ideas, your energy, and your courage. Step forward and make them count.

Let's keep growing. One bite at a time. The best is yet to come.

ACKNOWLEDGMENTS

I want to begin by thanking Justine Froelker and Amie Merz, two incredible women who have been nudging me for years to write a book. You saw something in me before I did, and your encouragement gave me the courage to share my voice with the world. I am deeply grateful for your belief in me.

A huge thank-you to Margo Dill, who generously shared her publishing wisdom and gave me a crash course in self-publishing. You helped me avoid countless missteps and made the process far less daunting. Your guidance was a true gift.

To my amazing group of advanced readers, Chrissy Ashford, Eric Fjone, Lauren Kuechenmeister, Barry Englehardt, Steph Auping, Brendan Dowd, Travis Gillison, Smaran Mandala, Lucas Merz, Liz Haberberger, Al Dea, Justine Froelker, Terence Bostic, Julie Winkle Giulioni, Megan Galloway, Rebecca Ellis, Charles Good, Diana Bentz, and Matt Homann, thank you for your thoughtful feedback, encouragement, and time. You helped shape this book into something I am proud of.

Special thanks to Todd Bauman. Your illustrations brought this book to life in a way I could not have imagined. You helped me create a book that feels playful, human, and real, and I am so grateful for your talent and collaboration.

To my wife, Susan, thank you for lending your design skills and artistic eye to the cover and layout. You made this book feel like me, and your support throughout this journey means everything.

And finally, to my dad, Raymon, thank you for encouraging me from a young age to pursue my passions, be unapologetically myself, and never compromise my dreams. Your voice has always been in my head, cheering me on.

ABOUT THE AUTHOR

Ryan McCrea helps leaders lead like humans. For over 20 years, he has worked at the intersection of learning, leadership, and behavior change, not just building programs, but building people. His approach is rooted in clarity, candor, and a deep belief that leadership isn't about having all the answers. It's about showing up with intention when it matters most.

Ryan has coached executives, facilitated hundreds of workshops, and led culture-shaping initiatives inside companies of all sizes. He is known for creating experiences that stick long after the slide deck is closed because they are real, relevant, and refreshingly honest. His work focuses on the messy, meaningful moments of work and leadership, including giving feedback, navigating conflict, and staying grounded when the pressure is on.

He writes the way he talks, clear, practical, and just a little witty. His insights have resonated with tens of thousands of professionals on LinkedIn, where he shares bite-sized lessons that help people show up with more purpose, presence, and heart. Quick Bites of Insight™ is a natural extension of that work, short, powerful reflections designed to meet people where they are, in the middle of their day, their inbox, or their next big decision.

Ryan lives in St. Louis with his wife, Susan, and their two cats, Zooey and Coco. When he's not helping others grow, he is probably deep in a conversation about music, movies, fashion, or pop culture, or juggling three tasks at once with a steaming cup of tea nearby.